Angela Sandler

Thermomix Cookbook

150

Delicious, easy and quick recipes

All rights reserved

ISBN : 9798848991659

Table of content

Starters 40

Main dishes........................66

Desserts 117

Cakes 143

Introduction

The German brand Vorwerk has been particularly noticed since the release of its Thermomix which, in a way, is the king of food processors. Although the versatility of the Moulinex i-Companion or i-Companion Touch XL robots and other competing devices may be preferred by users, Thermomix remains the undisputed market leader.

The latest, the Thermomix TM6, offers some new features compared to the younger TM5. Thus, the TM6 comes with a new appearance, equipped with a larger touch screen and new accessories. In addition, thanks to Wi-Fi, you will have access to the Cookidoo application which offers you many recipes. But you have to be a subscriber to enjoy all these benefits.

Thermomix TM6 is a cooking robot that can also perform other tasks. Indeed, it chops, mixes, slices, cooks, simmers, sears. But, unlike its main competitors, such as the Kcook Multi Smart from Kenwood or the Cook Expert XL from Magimix, it does not grate and does not know how to cut into slices. However, nothing changes with this new model, as the comfort of use is unanimous.

Thermomix TM6 or Thermomix TM5?
From Thermomix TM5 to Thermomix TM6, the German brand Vorwerk has made some changes. In terms of design, nothing really changes. The devices remain similar, even if there is a big difference in the size of the control screen and its tactile character. Indeed, the control screen of the Thermomix TM6 is in color and larger (6.8 inches) than that of the TM5 (4.3 inches).

The capacity of the original bowl remains the same 2.2 L. The integrated scale now weighs 1 gram for TM6 against 5 grams for TM5.

In addition, there is high temperature cooking now integrated into the TM6, which for this reason has its own accessories not compatible with TM5. Thus, TM6 offers a temperature range between 30 to 160°C against 30 to 120°C for TM5. Due to this, the accessories also change for their quality. These are able to withstand high temperatures. In addition to this, TM6 offers an anti-splash cover.

Fermentation
Make protein-packed yogurt, probiotic-rich kimchi, and proof dough using the Fermentation mode

Multi-Level Cooking
Lets you prepare multiple dishes at the same time

Emulsify
Turn simple, clean ingredients into creamy homemade salad dressings

Slow-Cooking
Set and forget with Slow-Cooking mode, tenderizing any cut of meat and intensifying flavors in your dishes

Easy Clean-up
Clean-up is a breeze with dishwasher-safe parts and the residue-removing in the Pre-Cleaning mode

Smart at Heart
Smart at Heart, the Thermomix® TM6® automatically connects and updates its software over wi-fi, keeping your features up to date

Innovative and Intuitive
An intuitive user interfaces lets you tap your way to endless recipe inspiration with seamless Cookidoo® access and a 6.8" full-color touchscreen

Vapor and Aroma
The most flavorful, efficient way to steam healthy veggies and proteins

Sous Vide
Add to your culinary repertoire with Sous Vide mode. The technique popularized by professional chefs lets you perfectly cook vegetables, eggs, and fish

Whip & Whisk
Whip eggs, cream and more with the Butterfly Whisk

Sauté, Brown & Caramelize
Cook with precision thanks to integrated sensors and the High Heat Mode that maintain a constant, precise temperature

Weigh
No more hunting for the right measuring cup – weigh ingredients into the Mixing Bowl using the integrated digital scale

Stir, Mix, Blend, Chop, Grind, and Knead
The state-of-the-art blade rotates forward with a sharp edge to blend, chop, and grind, and a backward blunt edge to stir and knead

Varoma lid

Varoma tray

Varoma

The Thermomix® Varoma provides a gentle, easy way to steam fresh vegetables, meats and bread.

Varoma

Mixing Bowl Lid

The lid of Thermomix® is an integral part of the built-in safety measures. It must be in place for the locking arms to close around it and for the appliance to start. It also allows oil to be drizzled into mayonnaise at the perfect speed.

Splash guard

Measuring cup

Mixing bowl lid

Mixing Knife

The multi-purpose efficient mixing knife is the heart of Thermomix®. It stirs at low speeds, mixes at medium speeds (2 – 4) and chops at higher speeds. The rotation can be reversed for more gentle stirring, or shredding.

Butterfly Whisk

Simmering basket

Mixing bowl

Simmering Basket

Food cooked in the simmering basket is held clear of the rotating knife for perfect steaming or boiling, and the lid closes over it, for additional safety.

Scale

When precision and accuracy are required, Thermomix® won't let you down with its built-in digital weighing scale.

Mixing knife

Spatula

Use to scrape down the sides of mixing bowl, safely remove the simmering basket, and to assist with mixing or chopping through hole in mixing bowl lid.

Butterfly Wisk

The butterfly whisk is used to aerate sauces and mousses, whip egg whites and cream or make your own butter.

Splash Guard

The splash guard protects against splashing of hot content when cooking at higher temperatures, such as 320°F.

Mixing Bowl

Thermomix® has a durable stainless steel mixing bowl, with integrated heating.

Heating System

The heating system ensures the highest standard of performance in Thermomix® when cooking.

All Thermomix® parts, except the main appliance, are dishwasher-safe.

Spatula

Thermomix®

New Cooking Functions
24-in-1 and growing

 Weighing

 Thicken

 Rice Cooker

 Sugar Stages

 Grating and Milling

 Cooking

 Precise Heating

 Caramelising

 Steaming

 Mixing and Emulsifying

 Kneading

 Enhanced Pre Clean

 Chopping

 Kettle

 Mincing

 Sous Vide

 High Temperature

 Stirring

 Slow Cooking

 Whipping

 Fermentation

 Blending

 Egg Boiler Mode

 Warm Up

Appetizers

1.Vanilla Cucumber Jam

Ingredients for 10 people:

- ✓ 500 g skinless and seedless cucumber, chopped,

- ✓ 1 vanilla pod,

- ✓ 400 g of sugar,

- ✓ 30 g of lemon juice

Preparation :

1. Start by putting the cucumber, the seeds of the vanilla pod, the sugar and the lemon juice in the bowl of your Thermomix.

2. Program at speed 4 for 5 seconds.

3. Then, place the basket on the lid and set at speed 1 for 30 minutes at Varoma temperature.

4. Pour into two sterilized jars and close them, then turn them upside down and leave to cool.

5. Serve and enjoy.

2.Pintxo Donosti

Ingredients for 6 people:

- ✓ 50 g of sweet chives,
- ✓ 250g crab sticks,
- ✓ 2 boiled eggs,
- ✓ 1 can of marinated tuna (well drained),
- ✓ 200g mayonnaise,
- ✓ 1 rustic bread (large slices of round bread or small slices of bread),

Preparation :

1. Start by putting the chives in the bowl of your Thermomix, then set to speed 5 for 3 seconds.

2. Scrape the sides with a spatula, then set again at speed 5 for 3 seconds.

3. Scrape down the sides again, then add the crab sticks and eggs to the bowl.

4. Program at speed 4 for 3 seconds.

5. Add the mayonnaise and the tuna, then program at speed 3 for 10 seconds.

6. Spread the preparation obtained on toast.

7. Serve and enjoy.

3. Goat cheese bites with zucchini and ginger jam

Ingredients for 8 people:

- ✓ 250g zucchini,

- ✓ 1 small goat cheese roll,

- ✓ toasted bread,

- ✓ Zucchini and ginger jam,

Preparation :

1. Start by washing the zucchini, then cut them into slices.

2. Place a slice of goat cheese on each slice of zucchini, then place a little jam on top.

3. Serve with toast and enjoy.

4.Shrimp Dip

Ingredients for 6 people:

- ✓ 50 g cooked and peeled prawns,

- ✓ 110g cheese spread,

- ✓ 90 g of mayonnaise,

- ✓ Lemon juice,

- ✓ Chives or coriander (optional),

Preparation :

1. Start by putting the prawns in the bowl of your Thermomix and set to speed 5 for 5 seconds. Check that there are no large chunks left.

2. Add the cheese spread, mayonnaise and a few drops of lemon juice, then set to speed 2 for 30 seconds.

3. Then add a pair of chopped chives or cornage, then program at speed 2 for 5 seconds.

4. Serve with grilled toast and enjoy.

5.Zucchini and ginger jam

Ingredients for 2 jars:

- ✓ 750 g zucchini,

- ✓ 1 large lemon,

- ✓ A piece of ginger about 2 cm,

- ✓ 300 g of sugar,

Preparation :

1. Start by peeling the lemon, removing the yellow and white skin, then put it in the bowl of your Thermomix.

2. Add 750 g of zucchini cut into pieces as well as the peeled pieces of ginger, then set to speed 5 for 10 seconds.

3. Then add the sugar and set at speed 2 for 45 minutes at 100°C, replacing the measuring cup with the basket to avoid splashing.

4. Once the time has elapsed, program at progressive speed 7-10 for 30 seconds.

5. Fill jars to the brim with the jam and cover them, then turn them upside down and let them cool.

6. Serve as an aperitif with toast and enjoy.

6. Cheese Roll with Bacon and Nuts

Ingredients for 8 people:

- ✓ 300g Philadelphia-style cream cheese
- ✓ 160 g of goat cheese,
- ✓ 60 g grated cheddar,
- ✓ 1/4 cup pistachios + 100g of bacon,
- ✓ 1/4 cup dried blueberries,
- ✓ 1/4 cup crispy fried onion (optional),
- ✓ 5 tablespoons of olive oil,

Preparation :

1. Start by putting 100 g of bacon cut into small pieces and 5 tablespoons of olive oil in the bowl of your thermomix.
2. Set at speed 1.5 for 15 minutes at Varoma temperature. You must have fried and crispy bacon if not, program a few more minutes at the same speed and temperature.
3. Remove the bacon from the bowl and drain the oil, then return the bacon to the bowl and run at speed 5.5 for 5 seconds. Remove and reserve in a bowl.
4. Without washing the bowl, put the dried blueberries and pistachio in it and set to speed 7 for 5 seconds.
5. Remove and mix with the bacon, then add the crispy fried onions and mix again.
6. Wash and dry the thermomix bowl and put the cream cheese, goat cheese and grated cheddar in it.
7. Program at speed 3.5 for 20 seconds.
8. Then place the resulting cheese mixture on a surface of aluminum foil. Form a roll and compact it using aluminum foil.
9. Once the shape is made, place in the freezer for 40 minutes.
10. Take the roll out of the freezer and unwrap it from the aluminum foil, then cover it with the bacon and nut mixture.
11. Serve immediately with slices of bread or chill in the fridge.
12. Treat yourself.

7.Savory Profiteroles Stuffed with Surimi and Tuna

Ingredients for 5 people:
- ✓ 300ml of water,
- ✓ 150 g of wheat flour,
- ✓ 100g of butter,
- ✓ Two pinches of salt + 4 eggs,

Topping:
- ✓ 8 crab sticks,
- ✓ 2 large pickled gherkins,
- ✓ 2 slices of leek,
- ✓ 80 g of tuna,
- ✓ 120 g cream cheese,
- ✓ 4 tablespoons of mayonnaise,

Preparation :
1. Start by putting 300 ml of water and 100 g of butter in the bowl of your thermomix, then set to speed 1 for 3 minutes at 110°C.
2. Add the wheat flour and the 2 pinches of salt and set at speed 3.5 for 30 seconds.
3. Remove the dough obtained and place it in a lard and looped pastry bag.
4. Preheat the oven to 180°C. Line a baking sheet with parchment paper.
5. Shape the profiteroles by placing them on the plate.
6. Bake at medium height at 180°C until you see that they are golden.
7. Wash and dry the thermomix bowl, then put in 8 crab sticks, the tuna, the 2 gherkins and the 2 slices of leek.
8. Program at speed 5 for 5 seconds.
9. Add cream cheese and mayonnaise, then turn to speed 1.5 for 30 seconds.
10. Once the profiteroles are finished cooking, remove them from the oven and let them cool for a few minutes.
11. Then, open them in half and fill them with the surimi and tuna filling.
12. Serve and enjoy.

8. Yogurt and mint sauce

Ingredients for 4 persons :

- ✓ 2 unsweetened yogurt,
- ✓ 1 clove of garlic,
- ✓ 2 pinches of salt,
- ✓ 2 pinches of sugar,
- ✓ 1 cup mint leaves,

Preparation :

1. Start by peeling the garlic clove, then put it in the bowl of your thermomix.

2. Add sugar, salt and mint leaves.

3. Program at speed 6 for 6 seconds.

4. Scrape the sides with a spatula, then set again at speed 6 for 6 seconds.

5. Add the yogurt and program at speed 2 for 6 seconds.

6. Taste and adjust the salt or sugar if necessary.

7. Place in the refrigerator until serving time.

8. Serve as an appetizer or side dish and enjoy.

9. Spicy lentils with Greek yogurt

Ingredients for 8 people:

- ✓ 250 g of lentils + 100 g onion in pieces,
- ✓ 1/2 zucchini in pieces + 1 chopped tomato,
- ✓ 1 chopped carrot + 2 cloves garlic,
- ✓ 1 teaspoon of paprika + 1 bay leaf,
- ✓ 780g of water + 1 teaspoon of cumin,
- ✓ 1 teaspoon of curry,
- ✓ Pepper to taste,
- ✓ salt to taste,
- ✓ 1 unsweetened Greek yogurt,
- ✓ 2 sprigs of mint, chopped mint (leaves only),
- ✓ 1 / 2 teaspoon of sugar,
- ✓ Juice of 1/2 lemon,

Preparation :

1. Start by soaking the lentils in water for at least 3 hours.
2. Put the onion, 1.5 cloves of garlic and olive oil in the bowl of your Thermomix.
3. Program at speed 4 for 4 seconds.
4. Scrape the sides with a spatula, then set at speed 1 for 6 minutes at varoma temperature.
5. Add the paprika and set at speed 1 for 1 minute at Varoma temperature.
6. Then add the drained lentils, carrot, zucchini, bay leaf, water, spices and salt, then set at spoon speed in reverse for 40 minutes at 100°C.
7. Put 1/2 clove of garlic as well as a pinch of salt and the mint in a mortar, then crush everything.
8. Add the yogurt, lemon juice and sugar, then mix everything together.
9. Divide the lentil preparation into a mini appetizer bowl and top with the yoghurt sauce.
10. Serve and enjoy.

10. Gazpacho with cucumber and grapes

Ingredients for 2 people:

- ✓ 300 g cucumber, peeled and seeded,
- ✓ 150 g seedless white grapes (and 4 grapes for decoration),
- ✓ 1 clove garlic, peeled,
- ✓ 1 tablespoon of sherry vinegar,
- ✓ 55g of water,
- ✓ 55g of milk,
- ✓ 40 g of extra virgin olive oil,
- ✓ Walnuts or pistachios,
- ✓ Salt and white pepper,

Preparation :

1. Start by putting the cucumber in pieces in the bowl of your Thermomix.

2. Add the garlic clove, seedless raisins, sherry vinegar, milk and water to the bowl.

3. Program at speed 8 for 1 minute.

4. Then set to speed 3 for 30 seconds, pouring the oil through the hole in the lid. Add salt and pepper.

5. Place in the refrigerator for at least 1 hour before serving.

6. Serve in two bowls or glasses and garnish with the grapes and some walnuts or pistachios.

7. Treat yourself.

11. Light Mojito Granita

Ingredients for 6 people:

- ✓ 40 cl of water,
- ✓ 60 g of sugar,
- ✓ Juice of 10 limes,
- ✓ Leaves of 2 bunches of chopped mint,
- ✓ 50 cl of rum,

Preparation :

1. Start by putting the water and the sugar in a saucepan, then bring to the boil.

2. Once the sugar has melted, remove the pan from the heat.

3. Add the lemon juice and mix well, then add the chopped mint.

4. Pour in the rum and mix again, then place the mixture in a shallow dish.

5. Place in the freezer for at least 4 hours.

6. Then scrape with a fork and serve in glasses.

7. Treat yourself.

12. Spicy chickpea snack

Ingredients for 2 people:

- ✓ 400 g of cooked chickpeas,
- ✓ 10 g of La Vera paprika,
- ✓ 5 g ground cumin,
- ✓ 5 g chili flakes,
- ✓ 10 g onion powder,
- ✓ 10 g garlic powder,
- ✓ 30g brown sugar
- ✓ 10g of salt,
- ✓ 20 g of olive oil,

Preparation :

1. Start by drying the chickpeas using paper or a clean kitchen towel. Then let them dry for 30 minutes.
2. Preheat the oven to 200°C.
3. Meanwhile, put the rest of the ingredients except the oil in the thermomix bowl.
4. Program for 15 seconds at speed 8. Remove and set aside.
5. After the drying time, place the chickpeas on a baking sheet lined with parchment paper.
6. Grill for 30 minutes or until golden and crispy.
7. During this process, mix the chickpeas by mixing them.
8. When done cooking, transfer the hot chickpeas to a large bowl and drizzle with the oil.
9. Then sprinkle in the spice mixture and toss until well coated.
10. Let them cool before serving.
11. Treat yourself.
12. You can store them in an airtight container.

13. Hummus with Yoghurt and Light Mint

Ingredients for 4 persons :

- ✓ 400 g of cooked chickpeas,
- ✓ 100 g of 0% natural yoghurt,
- ✓ 1 tablespoon of tahini,
- ✓ 1 clove of garlic,
- ✓ 10 mint leaves,
- ✓ Juice of half a lemon,
- ✓ 1 pinch of cumin,
- ✓ 1 tablespoon of olive oil,
- ✓ Salt and pepper,
- ✓ A little paprika to garnish (optional),

Preparation :

1. Start by putting all the ingredients in a blender.

2. Mix everything for a few minutes according to the desired texture.

3. If ever you find that the texture is too thick, add a little water and mix again.

4. Serve with a drizzle of olive oil and sprinkle with paprika.

5. Treat yourself.

14. Avocado hummus

Ingredients for 4 persons :

- ✓ 1 clove of garlic,

- ✓ 300g avocado,

- ✓ 400 g of cooked chickpeas,

- ✓ 30 g of olive oil,

- ✓ 1 dash of lemon juice,

- ✓ 1 pinch of ground cumin,

- ✓ Salt,

Preparation :

1. Start by putting all the ingredients in the bowl of your thermomix.

2. Program at progressive speed from 5 to 10 for 1 minute.

3. Transfer to a bowl and drizzle with olive oil, then refrigerate until ready to serve.

4. Serve and enjoy.

15. Hummus with beans and dried tomatoes

Ingredients for 4 persons :

- ✓ 200 g of cooked beans,

- ✓ 120g dried tomatoes in olive oil,

- ✓ 2 basil leaves,

- ✓ 40 g of olive oil (that of the tomatoes),

- ✓ 1 pinch of salt,

- ✓ 2 small pieces of ground white pepper,

- ✓ 1 pinch of smoked paprika,

Preparation :

1. Put all the ingredients in the thermomix bowl and set for 45 seconds at speed 5.

2. Scrape the sides with a spatula, then set for about 15 seconds at the same speed.

3. Serve your hummus immediately or store it in the fridge until ready to serve.

4. Treat yourself.

16. Light Coconut Oil Fried Bananas

Ingredients for 2 people:

- ✓ 2 medium, not very ripe bananas

- ✓ ½ teaspoon of ground cinnamon,

- ✓ 1 tablespoon virgin coconut oil (or unsalted butter),

Preparation :

1. Start by cutting the bananas into slices and sprinkle them with cinnamon.

2. Heat a large skillet over medium heat for about 3 minutes.

3. Add the coconut oil and stir to coat the entire pan.

4. Add the banana slices and cook for 2 to 3 minutes on each side until golden brown.

5. Divide between two plates, pouring the remaining coconut oil from the pan over the top.

6. Serve and enjoy.

17. Toasts with Ham Zucchini and Pesto

Ingredients for 6 servings:

For the pesto:
- ✓ 30 g of parmesan,
- ✓ 15 g of basil,
- ✓ 20 g of pine nuts,
- ✓ 1 clove of garlic,
- ✓ 50 g of olive oil,
- ✓ Salt,

For the rest of the toast:
- ✓ 6 medium slices,
- ✓ Sprockets,
- ✓ 6 thin slices of zucchini,
- ✓ 6 slices of ham,

Preparation :

1. Start by toasting the bread slices in a toaster while you prepare the rest of the recipe.
2. In a skillet without oil, lightly brown the pesto pine nuts as well as those you will use to decorate. Remove and set aside.
3. Put the cheese in the bowl of the thermomix and set for 15 seconds at speed 10.
4. Add the garlic, the basil leaves, the oil, the salt and only 20 g of pine nuts that you have grilled, the rest reserve it until the end of the recipe.
5. Program for 15 seconds at speed 7. Remove the resulting pesto and set aside in a bowl.

For mounting :

1. On the already grilled slices, spread a generous layer of pesto.
2. Spread the thin slices of zucchini and also the slices of ham over the pesto.
3. Decorate with the toasted pine nuts set aside previously.
4. Put the toasts on a platter and serve.
5. Treat yourself.

18. Endives Stuffed with Salad

Ingredients for 8 people:

- ✓ 8 endive leaves,
- ✓ 200 g peeled and chopped vegetables (potato, carrot, pea, sweet corn, etc.),
- ✓ 10 green olives,
- ✓ 1 can of tuna,
- ✓ 2 eggs,
- ✓ 50 g of mayonnaise,
- ✓ 20 g of mustard,
- ✓ Salt,

Preparation :

1. Fill the glass with 800 g of water, add a generous pinch of salt and place the basket with the eggs inside.
2. Close and put the Varoma in place with the chopped vegetables. Program for 20 minutes at Varoma temperature at speed 3.
3. Meanwhile, mix the mayonnaise and mustard in a bowl until both ingredients are incorporated.
4. Separate, wash and dry the endive leaves. Drain the tuna and set aside. Cut the olives into slices and set aside.
5. After the time has elapsed, carefully remove the Varoma. Cool the vegetables to cut the cooking. Also cool the cooked eggs and peel them.
6. Chop one of the eggs and mix it with the vegetables and the tuna. Add the mayonnaise mixture and stir so that all the ingredients are coated with the sauce.
7. Fill the endive leaves with the mixture. Grate the remaining egg and spread it over the endives. Finish the decoration with the sliced olives.
8. Store in the fridge until ready to serve.
9. Treat yourself.

19. Zucchini Dip

Ingredients for 6 people:

- ✓ 500 g of organic zucchini,
- ✓ Olive oil,
- ✓ 25 g tahini pasta,
- ✓ The juice of 1/2 or 1 lemon (according to taste),
- ✓ white pepper,
- ✓ Pumpkin and/or sunflower seeds,

Preparation :

1. Start by preheating the oven to 200°C.
2. Wash the zucchini and cut them into thick slices, then put them in a baking dish and drizzle olive oil on top.
3. Bake for 30 to 45 minutes at 200°C until the zucchini are cooked.
4. Take the zucchini out of the oven and let them rest for 10 minutes, then put them in the bowl of your Thermomix.
5. Add the tahini paste, the juice of 1/2 lemon, a little salt and pepper to the bowl.
6. Program at progressive speed from 4 to 7 for 10 seconds.
7. Taste and add a little salt if needed, then if you want more lemon flavor add the juice of 1/2 a lemon or 15g water.
8. Program at progressive speed from 5 to 8 for 10 seconds.
9. Transfer the preparation to a bowl and grind a little white pepper on the surface, then add a little olive oil.
10. Decorate with pumpkin or sunflower seeds, then serve with corn chips.
11. Treat yourself.

20. Watermelon Gazpacho

Ingredients for 6 people:

- ✓ 500 g of watermelon,
- ✓ 500 g ripe tomatoes, cut into pieces,
- ✓ 60 g of cucumber in pieces,
- ✓ 80 g of red pepper in pieces,
- ✓ 1 clove of garlic,
- ✓ Salt,
- ✓ 2 tablespoons of vinegar,
- ✓ 4 tablespoons of virgin olive oil,

Preparation :

1. Start by putting all the ingredients except the olive oil in the bowl of your Thermomix.

2. Program at speed 5 for 1 minute.

3. Then, program at progressive speed from 1 to 2 for 1 minute 30 seconds.

4. Add olive oil and set to Turbo mode for 2 seconds.

5. Place in the refrigerator until serving time.

6. Serve and enjoy.

21. Light Spirulina Guacamole

Ingredients for 4 persons :

- ✓ 2 very ripe avocados,

- ✓ 1 teaspoon of spirulina powder,

- ✓ 1 tomato cut into small dice,

- ✓ ½ chopped onion,

- ✓ Juice of ½ lemon,

- ✓ 1 good sprig of cilantro, chopped

- ✓ 1 pinch of chili powder,

- ✓ Salt and pepper,

Preparation :

1. Start by peeling the avocados, then pit them and mash the flesh using a fork.

2. Add the lemon juice, onion, tomato, spirulina, chili, coriander, salt and pepper, then mix everything well.

3. Serve and enjoy.

22. Spinach turnovers

Ingredients for 4 Servings:

- ✓ 1 puff pastry,
- ✓ 150 g onions, halved,
- ✓ 1 clove of garlic,
- ✓ 10 g of olive oil,
- ✓ 400 g of fresh spinach,
- ✓ 50g of milk,
- ✓ 3 pinches of freshly ground pepper, to be adjusted according to taste,
- ✓ 30 g of pine nuts,
- ✓ 2 pinches of Espelette pepper, to be adjusted according to taste,
- ✓ 1 beaten egg,

✓ *Preparation :*

1. Place onions and garlic in mixing bowl then chop 5 sec/speed 5. Scrape down sides of mixing bowl with spatula.
2. Add olive oil and 400 g spinach, then cook 15 min/120°C/simmer speed.
3. Add the milk and cook 5 min/100°C/speed 1, without the measuring cup. Transfer to a container. Add the remaining 4 pinches of salt, pepper and pine nuts, then mix. Let the stuffing cool down before filling the turnovers.
4. Line 2 baking sheets with baking paper and set aside.
5. Roll out the puff pastry to a thickness of about 3 mm. Using a cookie cutter (Ø 10 cm), preferably fluted, cut out 18 pieces of dough, fill them with the spinach stuffing, then close them in half-moons by welding them edge to edge. Spread the turnovers on the prepared plates and refrigerate for 15 minutes. Meanwhile, preheat the oven to 180°C (Th. 6).
6. Brush the turnovers with the beaten egg using a pastry brush, then place in the oven and cook for 20-25 minutes at 180°C. Serve hot.

23. Small tuna plugs

Ingredients for 10 Servings:

- ✓ 180 g drained tuna,
- ✓ 50 g of tomato puree,
- ✓ 30g of milk,
- ✓ 90 g of grated cheese,
- ✓ 1 tbsp of mustard,
- ✓ 4 eggs,
- ✓ Parsley,
- ✓ 1 onion,
- ✓ Salt,
- ✓ Pepper,

Preparation :

1. Preheat your oven to 160°C.

2. Then, peel and cut the onion in 4, put it in the bowl of your thermomix with all the other ingredients, and mix 25 sec/speed 5.

3. Then pour the preparation obtained into small silicone molds. Put in the oven for 30min.

24. Light sesame cherry tomatoes

Ingredients for 6 people:

- ✓ 300 g of cherry tomatoes,

- ✓ 200 g of sugar,

- ✓ 100g of water,

- ✓ 50 g sesame seeds,

- ✓ 20 g of balsamic vinegar,

Preparation :

1. Start by heating the water with the sugar in a saucepan over medium heat.

2. As soon as the mixture thickens, add the balsamic vinegar and cook for a few minutes.

3. Pierce the cherry tomatoes with toothpicks.

4. Place the sesame seeds in a deep plate.

5. Dip the cherry tomatoes one by one in the caramel, then roll them in the sesame seeds.

6. Then place them on the parchment paper and let the caramel set for a few minutes.

7. Serve and enjoy.

25. Crab terrine with herbs

Ingredients for 8 servings:

- ✓ 250 g crab crumbs,

- ✓ 3 tablespoons chopped herbs (parsley, tarragon, chives),

- ✓ 4 eggs,

- ✓ 200g of milk,

- ✓ Salt and pepper,

Preparation :

1. Preheat the oven to 160°C.

2. In mixing bowl, add milk and eggs then mix 20 sec/speed 4.

3. Add crab crumbs, herbs, salt and pepper then mix 20sec/reverse/speed 3.

4. Pour the mixture into a terrine mold.

5. Bake in a bain-marie for 50 minutes.

6. Let cool before unmolding.

Starters

26. Zucchini carbonara

Ingredients for 8 Servings:

- ✓ 4 zucchinis,
- ✓ 800g of water,
- ✓ 1 onion cut in half,
- ✓ 200g diced ham,
- ✓ 10g of olive oil,
- ✓ 4 tablespoons of grated parmesan,
- ✓ 200g pasta (Konjac paste),

Preparation :

1. Wash the courgettes and cut them into tagliatelle using a vegetable peeler.

2. Add the water to the Thermomix then add the Varoma. Add the zucchini tagliatelle and cook 20 min/Varoma/speed 1.

3. Meanwhile, cook the Konjac noodles as directed on the package.

4. Drain the zucchini tagliatelle and the pasta.

5. Add the zucchini to the pan with the pasta and sauté for a few minutes. Reserve.

6. Meanwhile, add the onion to the Thermomix and mix 5 sec/speed 5. then scrape the sides of the bowl with the spatula. Add the diced ham and olive oil and cook 5 min/90°C/reverse/simmer.

7. Add the onion mixture to the skillet and sauté over low heat.

8. Serve with the parmesan on each plate.

27. Flavored carrots

Ingredients for 6 Servings:

- ✓ 600g carrots, cut into chunks,

- ✓ 1 tablespoon fresh coriander leaves, chopped

- ✓ 20 g of blanched almonds,

- ✓ 1 tablespoon orange blossom water,

- ✓ 3 tbsp. olive oil,

- ✓ 1 ½ tsp. lemon juice,

- ✓ ½ tsp. salt to be adjusted according to taste,

Preparation :

1. Place carrots, coriander and almonds in mixing bowl then chop 6 sec/speed 5. Scrape down sides of mixing bowl with spatula.

2. Add orange blossom water, olive oil, lemon juice and salt then mix 10 sec/speed 3.

3. Serve well chilled.

28. Tofu with sunny vegetables

Ingredients for 4 Servings:

- ✓ 2 onions,
- ✓ 1 clove of garlic,
- ✓ 10g of olive oil,
- ✓ 2 zucchinis,
- ✓ 2 eggplants,
- ✓ 100g of water,
- ✓ 1 tsp turmeric,
- ✓ Salt and pepper,
- ✓ 1 vegetable stock cube,
- ✓ 200 g of tofu,
- ✓ 2 tbsp soy sauce,

Preparation :

1. Place the halved onions in the thermomix bowl and the garlic clove then chop 5 sec/speed 5. Scrape down sides of bowl with spatula.

2. Add olive oil and cook 4min/100°C/reverse/speed 1.

3. Add the eggplant cut into cubes, the zucchinis cut into cubes, the water, the vegetable stock cube, the turmeric, the salt and the pepper then cook 15min/Varoma/reverse/Speed. Simmering.

4. Meanwhile, cut the tofu into pieces and add the soy sauce, marinate while the vegetables cook.

5. When the bell rings, add the tofu to the Thermomix bowl and cook 5min/Varoma.

29. Asian Broccoli and Romanesco Cabbage Salad

Ingredients for 4 Servings:

- ✓ 70 g dry roasted peanuts, salted,
- ✓ ½ bunch of fresh coriander + ½ bunch of fresh Thai basil,
- ✓ 10 sprigs of fresh chives, chopped + 500g of water,
- ✓ 300g broccoli, cut into florets,
- ✓ 300 g Romanesco cabbage, cut into florets,
- ✓ 10 g of fish sauce (nuoc-mâm),
- ✓ 1 C. powdered sugar + 10 g of soy sauce,
- ✓ 40 g of sesame oil + 15 g of rice vinegar,
- ✓ 25 g mirin + ½ small fresh red pepper, seeded,

Preparation :

1. Place peanuts in mixing bowl and chop 2 sec/speed. 7. Transfer to a container and set aside.
2. Place cilantro, Thai basil and chives in mixing bowl then chop 3 sec/speed. 7. Transfer to a bowl and set aside.
3. Then, put the water in the bowl, put the Varoma in place and put the broccoli and Romanesco cabbage florets in it, then steam 20 min/Varoma/speed. 1. Remove the Varoma and pass the cabbage under running cold water to stop the cooking. Transfer to the salad bowl with the chopped herbs, then set aside. Clean the bowl.
4. Place nuoc-mâm sauce, sugar, soy sauce, sesame oil, rice vinegar, mirin and red chili in mixing bowl then blend 10 sec/speed. 7.
5. Transfer the vinaigrette to the salad bowl with the cabbage and herbs, mix gently, then serve this salad with chopped peanuts.

30. Tabbouleh of quinoa with prawns and kiwis

Ingredients for 4 Servings:

- ✓ 800g of water,
- ✓ 4 pansies of salt,
- ✓ 200 g of quinoa,
- ✓ 2 lemons, peeled raw,
- ✓ 10 fresh mint leaves,
- ✓ 40 g of olive oil,
- ✓ 2 kiwis, cut in six,
- ✓ 300 g tomatoes, diced,
- ✓ 1 pinch of salt,
- ✓ 400g cooked prawns, peeled, halved,

Preparation :

1. Put the water and 4 pinches of salt in the bowl, then bring to the boil 8 min/Varoma/Vit. 1.
2. Add the quinoa and cook 12 min/100°C/reverse/speed. simmering. Drain the quinoa in the simmering basket then transfer to a bowl. Wipe the bowl.
3. Place lemons and mint in mixing bowl then blend 10 sec/speed. 10. Scrape down sides of bowl with spatula.
4. Add quinoa, olive oil, kiwis, tomatoes and salt then mix 3 sec/speed. 5.
5. Transfer to a serving dish and refrigerate for 30 minutes.
6. When ready to serve, add the prawns. Serve as fresh.
7. Tip: Add a drizzle of olive oil or a little more lemon juice depending on your taste.
8. If necessary, add fresh herbs (parsley, basil, etc.) in step 1.

31. Carrot Quiche with Tuna

For the dough:
- ✓ 200 g of wheat flour, and a little for flouring,
- ✓ 80g lukewarm water,
- ✓ 20g of olive oil,

The filling:
- ✓ 500g of water,
- ✓ 4 pinches of salt,
- ✓ 500 g carrots, cut into sections (2 cm),
- ✓ 3 eggs,
- ✓ 80g of milk,
- ✓ 160 g of natural canned tuna,
- ✓ 3 pinches of ground pepper,

Preparation :

1. Put the flour, olive oil and 80 ml of lukewarm water in the bowl, then activate the dough mixer mode for 1 min. Transfer the dough onto a sheet of cling film, form a ball, wrap the dough, then set aside in the fridge.
2. Put the remaining 500 g of water in the bowl. Insert simmering basket and add carrots, then steam 20 min/Varoma/speed 1. Remove simmering basket and set aside. Empty the bowl.
3. Preheat the oven to 180°C (Th. 6). Butter and flour a tart pan, then set aside.
4. Unwrap the dough, roll it out on a floured work surface and line the prepared pan. Place the eggs, milk, tuna, 3 pinches of salt and 3 pinches of pepper in the bowl, then mix 20 sec/speed 4. Pour the quiche mixture over the tart base and evenly distribute the carrot sections.
5. Place in the oven and cook for 30 minutes at 180°C, watching for the coloring.

32. Chickpea and spinach salad

Ingredients for 4 Servings:

- ✓ 3 cloves of garlic,
- ✓ 1 onion,
- ✓ 10g of olive oil,
- ✓ 500g of fresh spinach,
- ✓ The juice of a lemon,
- ✓ 1 tsp paprika,
- ✓ 1 tsp cumin,
- ✓ 5 sprigs of chopped parsley,
- ✓ 1 pinch of chili,
- ✓ Salt,
- ✓ Pepper,
- ✓ 200g of chickpeas,

Preparation :

1. Put the garlic in the thermomix bowl and the onion cut in half then mix 5 sec/speed 5. Scrape down sides of bowl with spatula.

2. Add olive oil and cook 5min/100°C/speed 1. Set up the whisk.

3. Add spinach, lemon juice, paprika, cumin, parsley, chili, salt and pepper then cook 5min/Varoma/reverse/Speed. Simmering.

4. Then add the chickpeas and continue cooking 10 min/Varoma/reverse/speed 1.

5. Remove the whisk and transfer to a serving dish, refrigerate 1 hour before serving.

33. Leek and apple salad

Ingredients for 4 Servings:

- ✓ 3 leeks,
- ✓ 500g of water,
- ✓ 1 apple,
- ✓ 25g of chopped almonds,
- ✓ 1 tbsp olive oil,
- ✓ 2 tbsp apple cider vinegar,
- ✓ Salt,
- ✓ Pepper,
- ✓ Chopped parsley,

Preparation :

1. Put 500g of water in the thermomix bowl and add the simmering basket.

2. Add the sliced leeks to the simmering basket and cook 15min/Varoma/Speed 1.

3. Set aside and let cool.

4. Peel and cut the apple into cubes then put it with the cooled leeks in a salad bowl.

5. Add the olive oil, vinegar, salt, pepper and chopped parsley to the preparation and mix everything gently.

6. Add chopped almonds on top before serving.

34. Pumpkin and Kale soup

Ingredients for 6 Servings:

- ✓ 250 g kale,
- ✓ 300 g of pumpkin,
- ✓ 2 carrots,
- ✓ 1 leek,
- ✓ 1 cube of vegetable soup,
- ✓ 500g of water,
- ✓ 1 tablespoon mustard seeds,
- ✓ Salt,
- ✓ Pepper,

Preparation :

1. Put the kale in the bowl, having previously removed the central stem, add the pumpkin cut into cubes, the carrots cut into rings, the leek cut into small sections, the vegetable stock cube, the water, the mustard seeds, salt and pepper.

2. Cook 20min/100°C/reverse/speed 1.

3. Variation: You can leave the soup like this or blend for 1 minute, gradually increasing the speed to 9.

4. You can add a spoonful of fresh cream to make it smoother.

35. Butternut-hazelnut puree

- ✓ 60 g of hazelnuts,
- ✓ 60 g of almonds,
- ✓ 40 g of various dried fruits (raisins, etc.),
- ✓ 6 sprigs of fresh dill, stemmed,
- ✓ 400 g of water,
- ✓ 1 butternut squash, halved lengthwise and seeded,
- ✓ 4 tablespoons of hazelnut oil,
- ✓ 50 g of 35% fat liquid cream,
- ✓ 2 pinches of salt, to be adjusted according to taste,

Preparation :

1. Place the hazelnuts, almonds, dehydrated dried fruit and dill in the mixing bowl then chop 1 sec/speed 5. Transfer to a bowl and set aside.

2. Put the water in the bowl. Put the squash in the Varoma, set it up and steam 40 min/Varoma/speed 1. Remove the Varoma and set aside. Empty the bowl.

3. Using a spoon, hollow out the butternut squash without breaking the skin, then put the flesh in the bowl. Reserve the skin for finishing. Add the hazelnut oil, single cream and salt to the contents of the mixing bowl then blend 1 min/speed 4. Transfer to the hollowed-out squash and sprinkle with the mixture of dried fruits and chopped dill.

4. Serve hot.

36. Tabbouleh with tomatoes and roasted peas

Ingredients for 4 Servings:

- ✓ 200 g fresh or frozen peas,
- ✓ 100 g of semi-complete couscous,
- ✓ 1 fresh onion,
- ✓ 150 g of cherry tomatoes,
- ✓ Juice of 1 lemon,
- ✓ 1 tbsp olive oil,
- ✓ Fresh mint or parsley,
- ✓ 1 tsp of thyme,
- ✓ 1 tsp rosemary,
- ✓ Salt,

Preparation :

1. Preheat the oven to 180°C.
2. Put 200g of peas in a baking dish, add 1 tbsp of olive oil, 1 tsp of thyme and rosemary and salt. Put in the oven for 12min.
3. Then, put 100g of semolina in a bowl, 100g of water and salt, mix and leave to swell, set aside for 5min. Fluff the couscous with a fork. Put the lemon juice and 1 tbsp of olive oil and mix the couscous. Reserve.
4. In the Thermomix put 1 onion cut in half and mix 5 sec/speed 5. Transfer the contents of the Thermomix to the salad bowl. Put 1 green pepper cut into strips and 150g of cherry tomatoes cut in half in the salad bowl.
5. Add the peas. Finally put 3 sprigs of fresh chopped parsley in the salad bowl, serve chilled.

37. Grilled eggplant flavored with spices

Ingredients for 4 Servings:

- ✓ 4 eggplants,
- ✓ 2 cloves garlic,
- ✓ A piece of ginger,
- ✓ 1 tbsp curry,
- ✓ 1 tsp cumin,
- ✓ 1/2 tsp turmeric,
- ✓ 1/2 tsp coriander powder,
- ✓ 1 pinch of cayenne pepper,
- ✓ 1 pinch of salt,
- ✓ 40g of olive oil,
- ✓ 5 sprigs of basil,
- ✓ 3 sprigs of parsley,
- ✓ 2 tbsp sesame seeds,

Preparation :

1. Preheat the oven to 190°C.
2. Cut the eggplants in half lengthwise. Using a squared knife, the flesh and place them on a baking sheet, previously covered with parchment paper.
3. Put the garlic in the bowl of the Thermomix, the ginger, the curry, the cumin, the turmeric, the coriander, the pepper, the salt, the olive oil, the leaves of basil and parsley then mix 5 sec/speed .5.
4. Using a kitchen brush, brush the eggplants with the preparation.
5. Put in the oven for 40 minutes at 190°C.
6. Remove from the oven and sprinkle the eggplants with sesame seeds. You can roast them again for 5 minutes in the oven with the sesame seeds.
7. Add a few chopped basil leaves over the eggplants and serve.

38. Green pepper and carrot quinoa salad

Ingredients for 4 Servings:

- ✓ 200g carrots, cut into chunks,
- ✓ 35 g shallots,
- ✓ 1 C. mustard,
- ✓ 6 pinches of salt,
- ✓ 3 pinches of ground pepper,
- ✓ 30 g of extra virgin olive oil,
- ✓ 20 g of vinegar,
- ✓ 1200 g of water,
- ✓ 200 g of pre-cooked wheat/quinoa,
- ✓ 1 green bell pepper, diced,
- ✓ 4 eggs,

Preparation :

1. Place carrots, shallots, mustard, salt, pepper, olive oil and vinegar in mixing bowl then chop 5 sec/speed 5. Transfer to a bowl and set aside.
2. Place 800 g water, quinoa and salt in mixing bowl then cook 15 min/100°C/speed 1. Meanwhile, dice green pepper and transfer to salad bowl. Drain the quinoa using the simmering basket, run it under cold running water, then transfer it to the salad bowl with the vegetables.
3. Then, put the remaining 400 g of water in the bowl. Insert simmering basket and add eggs, then steam 12 min/Varoma/speed 1.
4. Remove the simmering basket and plunge the eggs into cold water for about ten minutes to stop the cooking.
5. Gently peel the eggs, cut them into pieces, then add them to the contents of the salad bowl.
6. Mix and serve chilled.

39. Pancakes with vegetables

Ingredients for 8 Pieces:

- ✓ 1 zucchini,
- ✓ 1 red onion,
- ✓ 10 basil leaves,
- ✓ 1 red pepper,
- ✓ 1 clove of garlic,
- ✓ Salt,
- ✓ Pepper,
- ✓ 1 egg,
- ✓ 20g of flour,

Preparation :

1. Preheat the oven to 180°C.

2. Put the zucchini cut into pieces, the red onion cut in four, the red pepper cut into pieces, the salt, the pepper and the basil leaves in the bowl of the thermomix then mix 5 sec/speed 4. Scrape down sides of bowl with spatula.

3. Add egg and flour then mix 20sec/reverse/speed 3.

4. Line a baking sheet with baking paper. Using a cookie cutter, make the patties until all the preparation is used up.

5. Put in the oven for 20 minutes at 180°C.

6. Serve hot or cold.

40. Broccoli flan with bacon

Ingredients 6 Servings:
- ✓ 500 g of broccoli,
- ✓ 100 g of bacon,
- ✓ 6 cherry tomatoes,
- ✓ 1 carrot,
- ✓ 2 eggs,
- ✓ 100g cottage cheese,
- ✓ 3 tsp of parmesan,
- ✓ Salt,
- ✓ Pepper,
- ✓ 1 tsp nutmeg,

Preparation :

1. Preheat the oven to 200°C.

2. In the thermomix bowl, put the broccoli cut into florets and cook 15min/Varoma/reverse/speed 1.

3. Then drain the broccoli and return it to the bowl. Add eggs, cottage cheese, salt, pepper, nutmeg and parmesan then mix 1min/speed 6 at speed 6.

4. Pour the preparation into individual molds or into a large buttered dish.

5. Add the bacon, the carrots cut into thin slices and the cherry tomatoes cut in half to the preparation.

6. Put in the oven for 20 minutes at 200°C.

41. Red pepper broccoli and pine nut salad

Ingredients for 6 Servings:

- ✓ 300 g broccoli, cut into florets,
- ✓ 150 g red bell pepper, cut into pieces,
- ✓ 100 g apple, quartered,
- ✓ 30 g pine nuts or 30 g sunflower seeds,
- ✓ 25 g of olive oil,
- ✓ 15 g raspberry vinegar or 15 g white balsamic vinegar,
- ✓ 1 tsp. honey,
- ✓ 1.5 tbsp. mustard,
- ✓ 1 tsp. salt,
- ✓ ½ tsp. ground black pepper,

Preparation :

1. Place broccoli, pepper, apple, pine nuts, olive oil, vinegar, honey, mustard, salt and pepper in a bowl, then blend 5 sec/speed. 4.

2. Serve at room temperature.

3. Variation: Replace the pine nuts with other types of nuts.

42. Thai shrimp salad

Ingredients for 6 Servings:

- ✓ 3 limes, zest and 60 g of juice,
- ✓ 30 g of olive oil, and 1 tbsp. soup for the prawns,
- ✓ 30 g of fish sauce (nuoc-mâm),
- ✓ 2 cloves garlic,
- ✓ 10 g fresh green chili, halved and deseeded,
- ✓ 30 g fresh ginger, cut into pieces,
- ✓ 300 g white cabbage, cut into 1.5 cm cubes,
- ✓ 150 g carrot, cut into 1.5 cm rounds,
- ✓ 100g spring onions, halved
- ✓ 3 sprigs of fresh coriander, stemmed,
- ✓ Salt,
- ✓ 12 large raw shrimp, unshelled,
- ✓ 60 g of pumpkin seeds,

Preparation :

1. Zest and juice the lemons, then add the zest and juice to the bowl. Add 40 g olive oil, nuoc-mam, garlic cloves, chili and ginger, mix 20 sec/speed 5.

2. Add the white cabbage, carrot, spring onions, coriander and salt, mix 10 sec/speed 4. Transfer the contents of the bowl to a container, place it in the fridge for 1 hour.

3. Shell the prawns. In a hot skillet, pour 1 tbsp. tablespoon of olive oil then cook the prawns for 4 to 5 minutes over medium heat.

4. Divide the salad then the prawns on plates, sprinkle with pumpkin seeds and serve.

43. Invisible Leek-Carrot Cake

Ingredients for 4 Servings:

- ✓ 1 shallot,
- ✓ 4 leeks,
- ✓ 3 carrots,
- ✓ 10g of olive oil,
- ✓ 2 eggs,
- ✓ 100 ml of skimmed milk,
- ✓ 40g of flour,
- ✓ 1/2 sachet of yeast,
- ✓ 100 g of cheese,
- ✓ Salt,
- ✓ Pepper,

Preparation :

1. In the thermomix bowl, put the shallot and mix 5 sec/speed 5.
2. Add the leeks cut into small sections and the carrots, peeled and cut into thin rings.
3. Add olive oil and cook 20min/100°C/reverse/speed 1.
4. Meanwhile, preheat the oven to 180°C.
5. When the bell rings, transfer the vegetables to a salad bowl.
6. Without rinsing the bowl, add the eggs, milk, flour, cheese, yeast, salt and pepper and mix 30sec/speed 4.
7. Add vegetables and stir 1 min/reverse/speed 3.
8. Transfer the preparation into a silicone mold and bake for 40 minutes at 180°C.
9. Variation: You can add diced ham or bacon bits.

44. Andalusian Gazpacho

ingredients for 6 people:

- ✓ 1 kg of ripe tomatoes,
- ✓ 1 green pepper,
- ✓ 3 tablespoons of olive oil,
- ✓ 1 cucumber,
- ✓ 1 new onion (or half an onion),
- ✓ 2 tablespoons of vinegar,
- ✓ 1 clove of garlic,
- ✓ 50 g of bread,
- ✓ 1 teaspoon of salt,
- ✓ 1 glass of water (optional),

Preparation :

1. Start by washing the tomatoes and the pepper, then cut them into large pieces.
2. Peel the cucumber and chop it, then peel the onion and cut it into wedges.
3. Put the vegetables in the bowl of your thermomix and add the salt, the vinegar and the peeled garlic clove.
4. Program at speed 10 for 3 minutes.
5. Add the oil and if you want to have a more liquid texture, add a glass of water, then set to speed 10 for 2 minutes.
6. Place in the fridge and let cool.
7. When ready to serve, stir and divide into glasses or bowls, then garnish with pieces of cucumber and a few croutons.
8. Treat yourself.

45. Onion cream

Ingredients for 16 servings:

- ✓ 1 kg onion in quarters,
- ✓ 50g of butter,
- ✓ A pinch of sugar,
- ✓ Half a teaspoon of dried thyme,
- ✓ 250ml of beer,
- ✓ 800ml of water,
- ✓ 200 ml of liquid cream,
- ✓ 4 egg yolks,
- ✓ Salt,

Preparation :

1. Start by putting the onions in the bowl of your thermomix, then set to speed 4 for 4 seconds.
2. Add the butter, sugar and thyme, then program at speed 1 for 10 minutes at Varoma temperature.
3. Then add 200 ml of beer and set at speed 1 for 3 minutes at Varoma temperature.
4. Add the water and salt, then program at speed 1 for 50 minutes at 100°C.
5. Wait a few minutes for the temperature to drop, then set to progressive speed 5-10 for 2 minutes. The cream should be fairly thin, otherwise strain it and return it to the bowl.
6. Just before serving, heat on speed 1 for 4 minutes at Varoma temperature.
7. Then add the liquid cream, the egg yolks and the rest of the beer, then set to speed 1 for 4 minutes at 90°C.
8. Serve immediately and enjoy.

46. Quiche without dough with tuna and carrots

Ingredients for 6 Servings:

- ✓ 4 carrots,
- ✓ 1 onion,
- ✓ 10 g of olive oil,
- ✓ 1 tbsp of Provencal herbs,
- ✓ Salt,
- ✓ Pepper,
- ✓ 1 can of tuna,
- ✓ 3 eggs,
- ✓ 15 cl of skimmed milk,
- ✓ 100 g of grated cheese,
- ✓ 2 tbsp. cornstarch,
- ✓ 2 pinches of nutmeg,

Preparation :

1. Preheat the oven to 180°C.
2. Put the carrots cut into sections and the onion cut in half in the Thermomix bowl and mix 20sec/speed 4.
3. Add the olive oil, Provencal herbs, cumin, salt and pepper then sauté 5min/Varoma/Reverse/Speed. Simmering.
4. Add the drained and crumbled tuna and stir 30sec/reverse/speed 2. Transfer to a silicone dish.
5. Without rinsing the bowl, add the eggs, milk, cornstarch and nutmeg and mix 30sec/speed 4.
6. Pour this preparation into the dish and sprinkle with grated cheese then put in the oven for 30 minutes at 180°C.

47. Pepper-goat pie

Ingredients for 8 Servings:

- ✓ 40 g semi-salted butter, and a little for the mold,
- ✓ 40 g chorizo, cut into pieces,
- ✓ 160 g of wheat flour, and a little for flouring,
- ✓ 1 pinch of salt, to be adjusted according to taste,
- ✓ 50g of water,
- ✓ 1 tsp. Dijon mustard,
- ✓ 250 g of goat's cheese in a log, cut into slices,
- ✓ 1 red bell pepper, cut into strips,
- ✓ 10 leaves of fresh basil,

Preparation :

1. Place butter, chorizo, flour, salt and water in mixing bowl then mix 30 sec/speed 4. Form a ball and wrap in cling film. Reserve 30 minutes in the fridge.

2. Preheat the oven to 180°C (Th. 6). Butter and flour a tart mold (Ø 24 cm), then set aside.

3. On a floured work surface, roll out the dough using a rolling pin and line the prepared pan. Brush the bottom with mustard, cover with slices of goat cheese, then strips of pepper.

4. Place in the oven and cook for 35-40 minutes at 180°C, watching the color and serve immediately, sprinkled with basil.

48. Zucchini and ham roll

Ingredients for 8 Servings:

- ✓ 3 eggs (separate the whites from the yolks),
- ✓ 50 g flour,
- ✓ 2 zucchinis,
- ✓ 10g of olive oil,
- ✓ 1/2 teaspoon baking powder,
- ✓ salt pepper,
- ✓ 100 g of ham,
- ✓ 200g Philadelphia,

Preparation :

1. Preheat the oven to 180°C.
2. Place the zucchini in the bowl and chop 5 sec/speed 5.
3. Add the olive oil, salt and pepper then set 4min/100°C/reverse/speed. Simmering.
4. When the bell rings, allow to cool then add the egg yolks, flour and baking powder and mix 30sec/reverse/Speed.3.
5. Pour the mixture into a salad bowl and set aside.
6. Wash and dry the bowl, insert the whisk then add the egg whites and beat them until stiff, mixing 5min/speed 3.5.
7. Incorporate the egg whites into the previous preparation then mix with a spatula.
8. Pour the dough into a baking sheet covered with parchment paper and bake for 15 minutes at 180°C.
9. Once cooked, turn out onto a damp cloth and carefully remove the parchment paper.
10. Spread the Philadelphia cheese then place the slices of ham and roll up loosely.
11. Wrap in cling film and refrigerate until ready to serve.

49. Oatmeal soup

Ingredients for 4 Servings:

- ✓ 1 onion,
- ✓ 1 tsp olive oil,
- ✓ 100g rolled oats,
- ✓ Chopped parsley,
- ✓ 1 leek,
- ✓ 800g of water,
- ✓ 1 vegetable stock cube,
- ✓ Salt,
- ✓ Pepper,

Preparation :

1. Place the onion, cut in half, in the thermomix bowl and mix 5 sec/speed 5. Scrape down sides of bowl with spatula.

2. Add olive oil, oat flakes, parsley, leek cut into small pieces and cook 5min/100°C/reverse/speed 1.

3. Add water, vegetable stock cube, salt and pepper then cook 25min/100°C/reverse/speed 1.

4. At the ringtone, mix 30sec/Vit.7.

5. Adjust the seasoning if necessary. Serve.

50. Hake Nuggets

Ingredients for 4 persons :

- ✓ 250 g skinless hake,
- ✓ 50 g of soft cheese (mild taste),
- ✓ 50g of milk,
- ✓ Olive oil
- ✓ 50 g of sandwich bread,
- ✓ A pinch of salt,
- ✓ A beaten egg,
- ✓ A little flour,

Preparation :

1. Start by removing the skin from the hake, then cut it into small pieces and put it in the bowl of your thermomix.
2. Program at speed 8 for 5 seconds.
3. Add the grated cheese, milk, sandwich bread and a pinch of salt, then set to speed 7 for 15 seconds.
4. Remove the resulting dough from the bowl and place it on a plate.
5. Then, shape nuggets and pass them through the flour, then through the beaten egg.
6. Heat a large amount of oil in a frying pan and fry your nuggets until lightly browned.
7. Once the nuggets are cooked, place them on absorbent paper to remove excess oil.
8. Serve and enjoy.

Main dishes

51. Bobotie (beef gratin)

Ingredients for 8 Servings:

The meat preparation:
- ✓ 40 g of white sandwich bread (1-2 slices),
- ✓ 125g of milk + 80 g onion, halved,
- ✓ 1000 g of minced beef (5% fat) + 50 g of raisins,
- ✓ 50 g of blanched almonds + 30 g of lemon juice,
- ✓ ½ tsp. teaspoon of salt, to be adjusted according to taste,
- ✓ 2 tbsp. curry powder + 6 pinches ground nutmeg,
- ✓ ½ tsp. freshly ground pepper, to be adjusted according to taste,
- ✓ 10 g of olive oil,

The cream:
- ✓ 100g of milk + 4 eggs + 3 pinches of salt, to be adjusted according to taste,
- ✓ 3 pinches of freshly ground pepper, to be adjusted according to taste,

Preparation :

The meat preparation:
1. Soak the bread in the milk, drain well, then set aside in a container.
2. Place onion in mixing bowl then chop 5 sec/speed 5.
3. Then scrape the sides of the bowl with the spatula.
4. Add minced meat, drained sandwich bread, raisins, almonds, lemon juice, salt, curry, nutmeg and pepper, then mix 30 sec/reverse/speed 4, helping you to the spatula. Next, heat the olive oil in a frying pan over high heat and sauté the contents of the bowl for 5-10 minutes.
5. Then, divide the meat into 8 cassolettes, then clean and dry the bowl carefully.

The cream:
1. Preheat the oven to 200°C (Th. 6-7).
2. Place milk, eggs, salt and pepper in mixing bowl then mix 15 sec/speed 5.
3. Spread the preparation in the cassolettes over the meat, then put in the oven and cook for 30 minutes at 200°C. Then serve immediately.

52. Vegetables stuffed with fish

Ingredients for 8 Servings:

- ✓ 20 g of hazelnuts,
- ✓ 20 g of breadcrumbs,
- ✓ 1 zucchini + 4 medium tomatoes,
- ✓ 1 red pepper + 70 g shallots,
- ✓ 10 g of olive oil,
- ✓ 1 tsp curry powder,
- ✓ 3 pinches of salt,
- ✓ 3 pinches of ground white pepper,
- ✓ 400 g haddock, cut into pieces,

Preparation :

1. Place hazelnuts and breadcrumbs in mixing bowl then chop 4 sec/speed 6. Transfer to a bowl and set aside.
2. Cut the zucchini into 4 cm sections, cut the tomatoes in half so as to obtain a hat, then cut the pepper in four. Hollow out the zucchini and tomatoes using a melon baller. Reserve the hollowed-out vegetables and their trimmings.
3. Place shallots in mixing bowl and chop 5 sec/speed 5. Scrape down sides of mixing bowl with spatula.
4. Add the olive oil and zucchini trimmings, then sauté 5 min/120°C/simmer speed, without the measuring cup.
5. Add tomato juice and blend 10 sec/speed 5.
6. Then add the curry, salt and pepper, then cook 5 min/105°C/speed 1, without the measuring cup.
7. Preheat the oven to 180°C (Th. 6). Line a baking sheet with baking paper and set aside.
8. Add the haddock pieces and cook 5 min/105°C/reverse/simmer speed. Fill the hollowed-out vegetables with the fish stuffing, sprinkle them with hazelnut breadcrumbs, then place them on the prepared baking sheet.
9. Put in the oven and cook for 20 minutes at 180°C.

53. Chicken with Cuban pineapple

Ingredients for 4 Servings:
- ✓ 100 g onion, halved + 30 g of olive oil,
- ✓ 4 chicken thighs, with bone and skin,
- ✓ 380g of water + 250 g pineapple in syrup, in pieces,
- ✓ 200 g of coconut milk + 30 g grated coconut,
- ✓ ½ tsp. salt + 2 pinches of ground pepper,
- ✓ 1 chili, split,

Preparation :
1. Place onion in mixing bowl and chop 5 sec/speed 5. Then scrape down sides of mixing bowl with spatula.
2. Add 10 g of olive oil, then sauté 5 min/120°C/simmer speed, without the measuring cup.
3. Meanwhile, cut the chicken thighs in half at the joint and brown them in a pan with the remaining 20 g of olive oil. When they are nicely colored, remove the chicken thighs, then put them in the Varoma. Moisten with 80 g of water and scrape the bottom of the pan with a wooden spoon to remove the juices.
4. Then, drain the pineapples over a container using a colander. Add 100 g of their syrup, the juice from the pan, the remaining 300 g of water, the coconut milk, the grated coconut, the salt, the pepper and the chili in the bowl, then set up the Varoma and steam 30 min/Varoma/speed 1. Then remove Varoma and chili and set aside.
5. Serve the chicken pieces with the pineapple and
6. Tips: You can accompany this dish with rice, to do this: Weigh the rice in the simmering basket, then rinse it under running cold water. Then, insert the simmering basket, put the Varoma back in place, add the drained pineapple.
7. Then steam 15 min/Varoma/speed 3. Serve the chicken pieces immediately with the rice and pineapple.

54. Salted ratatouille cobbler

Ingredients for 6 Servings:

- ✓ 300 g of wheat flour + 10 g baking powder,
- ✓ 2 tbsp. grated parmesan, and 1 tbsp. coffee,
- ✓ 3 pinches of salt + 25 g semi-salted butter, in small pieces,
- ✓ 4 tbsp. of natural yogurt, stirred,
- ✓ 50g of milk + 1 egg + 1 clove of garlic, peeled,
- ✓ 10g of olive oil + 1 yellow onion, peeled and cut 2,
- ✓ 1 small eggplant, sliced + 2 small zucchinis, sliced,
- ✓ 1 red bell pepper, sliced + 1 yellow bell pepper, sliced,
- ✓ salt and ground pepper + 2 tomatoes, sliced,

Preparation :

1. Start by preparing the cobbler dough. Put the flour, baking powder, 2 tbsp. tablespoon parmesan and salt in the bowl, then add the butter, yoghurt and activate the Kneader mode /1 min.
2. Then add milk and egg, then mix 10 sec/speed. 3.
3. Form a ball, then keep it in the fridge. Then wash and dry the bowl.
4. Place garlic and onion in mixing bowl then chop 5 sec/speed. 5. Then scrape the sides of the bowl with the spatula.
5. Then add the olive oil and sauté 3 min/120°C/reverse/speed. 2.
6. Add the zucchini, then cook 5 min/100°C/reverse/speed. 1.
7. Then add the peppers and zucchini. Season with salt and pepper, then simmer 15 min/100°C/speed 1.
8. Add tomatoes and continue cooking 5 min/100°C/speed 1.
9. Preheat the oven to 180°C, then transfer the ratatouille to an oven dish, removing a little cooking liquid if there is a lot.
10. Roll out the dough to a thickness of about 1 cm, then cut out discs of dough using a cookie cutter.
11. Place the circles of dough on the ratatouille, then sprinkle with the remaining parmesan and bake for 35 minutes. Taste quickly.

55. Ground beef curry with eggplant

Ingredients for 6 Servings:

- ✓ 2 onions,
- ✓ 2 cloves garlic,
- ✓ 10g of olive oil,
- ✓ 600 g ground beef 5%,
- ✓ 1 lemongrass stick,
- ✓ 1 tbsp turmeric,
- ✓ 1/2 red pepper,
- ✓ 1 tbsp cumin,
- ✓ 1 tbsp curry,
- ✓ 2 eggplants,
- ✓ 1 can of crushed tomatoes,
- ✓ 1 lime,
- ✓ 20 cl of water,
- ✓ Salt and pepper,

Preparation :

1. Put the onions cut in half in the thermomix bowl and the garlic then mix 5 sec/speed 5. Scrape down sides of bowl with spatula.
2. Add olive oil and cook 3min/90°C/reverse/speed 1.
3. Add the minced meat, lemongrass, chilli, turmeric, cumin, curry then cook 5 min/100°C/reverse/speed 1.
4. Then add the diced aubergines, crushed tomatoes, water, lime, salt and pepper then cook 20min/Varoma/reverse/Speed. Simmering. Check the cooking if not prolong.
5. Tip: You can accompany this dish with rice.

56. Stir-fried beef and beans

Ingredients for 4 Servings:

- ✓ 300g strip steak,
- ✓ 20g of oil,
- ✓ 2 minced garlic cloves,
- ✓ 1 red onion,
- ✓ 150 g flat beans,
- ✓ 150 g sliced mushrooms,
- ✓ 1 pinch of salt,
- ✓ 100g beef broth,

Marinade:

- ✓ 2 tsp shaoxing wine,
- ✓ 2 tsp light soy sauce,
- ✓ 1 pinch of black pepper,
- ✓ 2 tsp dark soy sauce,
- ✓ 2 tsp sesame oil,
- ✓ 1 pinch of salt,
- ✓ 2 teaspoons of cornstarch,

Preparation :

Marinade:

1. Add shadowing wine, soy sauce, dark soy sauce, sesame oil, pepper and cornstarch then mix 15sec/speed 3.
2. Place the steak on a plate and spread the marinade over it. Reserve 30min in the fridge.
3. Meanwhile, put the garlic in the bowl of the Thermomix and the red onion cut in half then mix 5 sec/speed 5. Scrape down sides of bowl with spatula.
4. Add the mushrooms cut into pieces, olive oil, salt and beef broth. Set up the Varoma and insert the green beans then cook 20min/Varoma/reverse/speed 1.
5. When the bell rings, place the meat and the marinade in the Thermomix bowl, put the Varoma back in place then cook 4 min/120°C/reverse/speed 1.

57. Asian Chicken Meatballs

Ingredients for 30 Pieces:

- ✓ 2 cloves garlic,
- ✓ 1 shallot, cut in half,
- ✓ 1 cm of fresh ginger,
- ✓ 2 carrots, halved,
- ✓ 1 bunch of fresh coriander,
- ✓ 1 freshly squeezed lime juice,
- ✓ 50 g of oyster sauce,
- ✓ 20 g of fish sauce (nuoc-mâm),
- ✓ 500 g chicken fillets, skinless, cut in three,
- ✓ 15 g of cornstarch,
- ✓ 1 egg,
- ✓ 50 g of white sesame seeds,

Preparation :

1. Preheat the oven to 200°C (Th. 6). Place garlic, shallot, ginger and coriander in mixing bowl then chop 4 sec/speed 7.

2. Add carrots and chop 5 sec/speed 5.

3. Add lime juice, oyster sauce, fish sauce, chicken, cornstarch and egg, then Turbo Blend/2 sec/2 times.

4. Form meatballs with the preparation and place them on a baking sheet lined with baking paper. Sprinkle them with sesame seeds, then put in the oven and cook for 15 minutes at 200°C.

5. Serve hot or cold with a chili sauce and green salad leaves.

58. Tabbouleh of quinoa with prawns and kiwis

Ingredients for 4 Servings:

- ✓ 800g of water,
- ✓ 4 pansies of salt,
- ✓ 200 g of quinoa,
- ✓ 2 lemons, peeled raw,
- ✓ 10 fresh mint leaves,
- ✓ 40 g of olive oil,
- ✓ 2 kiwis, cut in six,
- ✓ 300 g tomatoes, diced,
- ✓ 1 pinch of salt,
- ✓ 400g cooked prawns, peeled, halved,

Preparation :

1. Put the water and 4 pinches of salt in the bowl, then bring to the boil 8 min/Varoma/Vit. 1.
2. Add the quinoa and cook 12 min/100°C/reverse/speed. simmering. Drain the quinoa in the simmering basket then transfer to a bowl. Wipe the bowl.
3. Place lemons and mint in mixing bowl then blend 10 sec/speed. 10. Scrape down sides of bowl with spatula.
4. Add quinoa, olive oil, kiwis, tomatoes and salt then mix 3 sec/speed. 5.
5. Transfer to a serving dish and refrigerate for 30 minutes.
6. When ready to serve, add the prawns. Serve as fresh.
7. Tip: Add a drizzle of olive oil or a little more lemon juice depending on your taste.
8. If necessary, add fresh herbs (parsley, basil, etc.) in step 1.

59. Half-cooked veal with chanterelles and vegetables

Ingredients for 4 Servings:

- ✓ 35 g of shallot,
- ✓ 10 g of olive oil,
- ✓ 100g of cleaned chanterelles,
- ✓ 100g of milk,
- ✓ 500g of water,
- ✓ 1 chicken stock cube,
- ✓ 300 g squash, in small cubes,
- ✓ 250g carrots, diced
- ✓ 4 sprigs of fresh thyme,
- ✓ salt and ground pepper,
- ✓ 500 g veal fillet, in large cubes,
- ✓ 1 tablespoon of cornstarch,

Preparation :

1. Prepare the sauce. Place shallot in mixing bowl and chop 5 sec/speed 5. Scrape down sides with spatula.
2. Add olive oil and sauté 3 min/110°C/speed 1.
3. Set up the whisk and add the drained mushrooms, 50g of milk, the water and the stock cube. Cook 20 min/110°C/reverse direction/simmer speed, without the measuring cup.
4. Place the squash, carrots and thyme in the Varoma lined with baking paper. Season with salt and pepper then close the paper in foil. Install Varoma and cook 15 min/110°C/reverse/simmer speed.
5. Arrange the veal on the platter, season with salt and pepper. Add the milk and cornstarch to the bowl. Insert tray and cook 17 min/110°C/reverse/simmer speed.
6. Serve the veal with the chanterelle mushroom sauce and the vegetables from the foil. Adjust the seasoning if necessary.

60. Spicy bulgur with green beans

Ingredients for 4 Servings:

- ✓ 500g of water,
- ✓ 200 g of bulgur,
- ✓ 1 kubor + 500g of green beans,
- ✓ 400 g of tomato sauce,
- ✓ 2 tbsp tomato puree,
- ✓ 2 shallots + 1 clove of garlic,
- ✓ 1 tsp curry + 10g of olive oil,
- ✓ 1 tsp paprika,
- ✓ 1 tsp coriander,
- ✓ Salt and pepper,

Préparation :

1. Put 500g of water in the bowl of the thermomix and the kubor, put the bulgur in place, weigh the necessary quantity and pass the bulgur under water. Then place the simmering basket in the thermomix bowl.
2. Position the Varoma and insert the green beans into the Varoma. Cook 15min/Varoma/Speed 1.
3. When the bell rings, remove the Varoma and the simmering basket and keep warm. Empty the thermomix bowl.
4. Put the shallots and the clove of garlic in the bowl of the thermomix then mix 5 sec/speed 5. Scrape down sides of bowl with spatula.
5. Add olive oil and sauté 4min/95°C/reverse/speed 1.
6. Add the curry, paprika, coriander, salt, pepper, tomato sauce and tomato puree then cook 10min/100°C/reverse/speed simmer.
7. Then, add the bulgur and the beans to the Thermomix bowl and cook 5min/100°C/reverse/speed. Simmering.
8. Serve hot.

61. Merguez pasta gratin

Ingredients for 4 Servings:

- ✓ 2 onions, quartered
- ✓ 1 clove of garlic,
- ✓ 1 red bell pepper, diced
- ✓ 10g of olive oil,
- ✓ 250g of milk,
- ✓ 300g of water,
- ✓ 1 tbsp tomato puree,
- ✓ Salt and pepper,
- ✓ 300 g of dry pasta,
- ✓ 240 g of merguez sausage,
- ✓ 150 g goat cheese cut into pieces,
- ✓ Variation: Add 50 g of pitted black olives, cut into rings,

Preparation :

1. Preheat the oven to 175°C.
2. Put the onion and the clove of garlic in the thermomix and mix 5 sec/speed 5.
3. Add pepper and olive oil and sauté 3min/120°C/speed 1.
4. Add the milk, water, tomato purée, salt and pepper to the Thermomix and cook 5min/10°C/speed 2.5.
5. Put the pasta and 240g of merguez cut into pieces in a gratin dish.
6. Pour the contents of the Thermomix bowl over the pasta (uncooked).
7. Add the goat cheese cut into pieces in the gratin dish.
8. Put in the oven for 40min at 175°C.

62. Pan-fried Chinese cabbage with green beans and soft-boiled egg

Ingredients for 4 Servings:

- ✓ 1 chinese cabbage,
- ✓ 200g of green beans,
- ✓ 1 onion,
- ✓ 200g ham matchsticks,
- ✓ 2 tbsp. soy sauce,
- ✓ 1 tablespoon sesame oil,
- ✓ 1 tablespoon olive oil,
- ✓ sesame seeds,
- ✓ 4 eggs + Salt + Pepper,

Preparation :

1. Place the halved onion in the thermomix bowl and mix 5sec/speed 5. Scrape down sides of bowl with spatula.

2. Add olive oil and sauté 3min/100°C/speed 1.

3. Add the shredded Chinese cabbage, green beans, sesame oil and soy sauce. Cook 10min/Varoma/reverse/speed 1.

4. Add the ham sticks, salt and pepper and cook 5min/Varoma/reverse/speed 1.

5. Meanwhile, cook the soft-boiled eggs in a pan of boiling water (cooking time: 5min).

6. Serve the Chinese cabbage with the beans, arrange the soft-boiled egg and sprinkle the dish with sesame seeds.

63. Haddock papillote with cabbage and squash

Ingredients for 4 Servings:

1. 800 g of water,
2. 400 g kale, cut into strips,
3. 240 g winter squash, cut into cubes,
4. 40 g shallots, halved,
5. 2 tbsp. fresh tarragon leaves,
6. 50 g of milk,
7. 6 pinches of salt, to be adjusted according to taste,
8. 6 pinches of ground pepper, to be adjusted according to taste,
9. 4 haddock fillets (approx. 600 g),

Preparation :

1. Put 400 g of water in the bowl. Insert the simmering basket and add the cabbage. Place Varoma in place and add squash, then steam 15 min/Varoma/speed 1. Remove simmering basket and Varoma. Empty the bowl.
2. Place shallots and tarragon in mixing bowl then chop 5 sec/speed 5. Scrape down sides of mixing bowl with spatula.
3. Add milk, 2 pinches of salt and pepper, then heat 5 min/80°C/speed 1.
4. Add the cooked cabbage and mix 20 sec/speed 2. On a sheet of baking paper, put ¼ of the squash, ¼ of the cabbage, 1 haddock fillet, sprinkle with a pinch of salt and pepper, then close the foil. Make 4 papillotes and divide them between the Varoma and the steam tray.
5. Place the remaining 400 g of water in the mixing bowl, set up the Varoma set and steam 15 min/Varoma/speed 2.
6. Serve immediately.

64. Stewed green beans, minced meat and tomatoes

Ingredients for 4 Servings:

- ✓ 2 onions,
- ✓ 3 cloves of garlic,
- ✓ 10 g of olive oil,
- ✓ 500 g of green beans,
- ✓ 500 g minced meat,
- ✓ 400 g of peeled tomatoes,
- ✓ 15g of lemon juice,
- ✓ 1 tsp ras el hanout,
- ✓ 1 tsp of 4 spices,
- ✓ Salt,
- ✓ Pepper,
- ✓ 300ml of water,
- ✓ 1 square of vegetable broth,

Preparation :

1. Place onions and garlic in mixing bowl then chop 5 sec/speed 5. Scrape down sides of mixing bowl with spatula.
2. Put the green beans in the Varoma and set aside.
3. Add the olive oil and brown 5 min/120°C/speed 1, without the measuring cup.
4. Add the tomatoes, lemon juice, minced meat, ras el hanout, 4 spices, salt, pepper and water.
5. Set up the Varoma and cook 25min/Varoma/reverse direction/Simmering speed.
6. Mix the beans with the tomato sauce.
7. Tip: You can also accompany this dish with rice.

65. Provencal vegetable gratin

Ingredients for 4 Servings:

- ✓ 2 onions,
- ✓ 1 clove of garlic,
- ✓ 10g of olive oil,
- ✓ 3 tomatoes,
- ✓ 3 zucchinis,
- ✓ 2 eggplants,
- ✓ 1/2 log of crumbled fresh goat cheese,
- ✓ Salt and pepper,
- ✓ Thyme,
- ✓ Rosemary,

Preparation :

1. Preheat the oven to 180 C.
2. Put the onion and the clove of garlic in the thermomix and mix 5 sec/speed 5.
3. Add olive oil and brown 5min/Varoma/Vit.2.
4. Peel and cut the zucchini, eggplants and tomatoes into slices.
5. Place all the vegetables in a gratin dish: a layer of eggplants, then a layer of zucchinis, then a layer of tomatoes. Finally, arrange the goat cheese cut into slices. Season with salt and pepper to taste then sprinkle with rosemary and thyme.
6. Bake for 50 mins. When your gratin is well browned and the vegetables are well cooked.
7. Serve immediately.
8. Variation: You can add a few spoonfuls of fresh cream between the vegetables.

66. Dahl of broccoli and cauliflower lentils

Ingredients for 4 Servings:

- ✓ 220 g onions, cut into 1 cm pieces,
- ✓ 2 cloves garlic,
- ✓ 2 cm fresh ginger, cut into pieces,
- ✓ 10 g of olive oil,
- ✓ 1 tsp. ground coriander,
- ✓ 1 tsp. powdered garam masala,
- ✓ 30 g of mustard seeds,
- ✓ 300 g of coral lentils,
- ✓ 200 g of coconut milk,
- ✓ 300 g of vegetable stock,
- ✓ 200 g of tomato coulis,
- ✓ salt and ground pepper,
- ✓ 250 g broccoli, cut into florets,
- ✓ 250 g of cauliflower florets,
- ✓ the juice of a lemon,
- ✓ 2 sprigs of fresh coriander, stemmed and chopped,
- ✓ 50 g puffed rice cakes, crushed,

Preparation :

1. Place onions, garlic and ginger in mixing bowl, chop 5 sec/speed 5. Scrape down sides of mixing bowl with spatula.
2. Add the oil, coriander, garam massala and mustard seeds, sauté 5 min/120°C/speed 1 without the measuring cup.
3. Add the lentils, coconut milk, vegetable broth, tomato coulis, salt and pepper. Put the cauliflower and broccoli in the Varoma, install it then cook 12 min/110°C/speed 1.
4. Transfer the cauliflower and broccoli to the bowl, add the lemon juice, cook 7 min/100°C/reverse/speed 1. Transfer the lentil dahl to a serving dish. Sprinkle with chopped cilantro and crushed rice cakes and serve hot.

67. Garlic and parsley seafood quiche

Ingredients for 8 Servings:

The shells:
- ✓ 60 g shallots, halved + 2 cloves garlic + ½ bunch of fresh parsley, stemmed,
- ✓ 10 g of olive oil + 350 g of frozen seafood cocktail + 50 g of dry white wine,
- ✓ 30g of milk + 1 egg,

The quiche:
- ✓ 200 g of wheat flour, and a little for flouring + 80g lukewarm water,
- ✓ 20g of olive oil + ½ tsp. salt,

Preparation :

The shells:
1. Place shallots, garlic and parsley in mixing bowl then chop 5 sec/speed 5. Scrape down sides of mixing bowl with spatula.
2. Add the olive oil and the frozen seafood, then sauté 10 min/120°C/simmer speed, without the measuring cup. Add the white wine and milk, then reduce 10 min/98°C/simmer speed, without the measuring beaker.
3. Then, filter the contents of the bowl using the simmering basket, taking care to collect the juice in a container, then let the contents of the simmering basket cool down. Place juice and egg back into mixing bowl then mix 10 sec/speed 4. Transfer to a bowl and set aside, then clean mixing bowl.

The quiche:
1. Put the flour, oil, salt and water in the bowl, then activate the mixer mode for 1 min. Remove the dough from the bowl and form a flattened ball, wrap in cling film, then refrigerate for 20 minutes.
2. Preheat the oven to 180°C (Th. 6). Butter and flour a tart mold (Ø 20-22 cm), then set aside.
3. Place the dough on a floured work surface, then roll it out with a rolling pin. Fill the prepared mold with it, then refrigerate for 15 minutes.
4. Garnish the quiche with the seafood, cover with the egg cooking juices. Put in the oven and cook for 35 minutes at 180°C. Serve hot, possibly accompanied by a green salad.

68. Pasta gratin with pear and blue broccoli

Ingredients for 4 Servings:

- ✓ 40 g parmesan, cut into pieces + 1500 g of water,
- ✓ 500 g broccoli, cut into florets + 135 g dry pasta,
- ✓ 300 g pears, cut into pieces + 35 g butter, cut into pieces,
- ✓ 35 g of wheat flour + 370 g of milk,
- ✓ 3 pinches of salt and pepper to adjust according to taste,
- ✓ 3 pinches of freshly grated nutmeg, to be adjusted according to taste,
- ✓ 125 g blue-veined cheese (bleu d'Auvergne, bleu des Causses, roquefort or fourme d'Ambert),

Preparation :

1. Place parmesan in mixing bowl and grate 5 sec/speed 10, then transfer to a bowl and set aside.
2. Put the water in the bowl, then place the Varoma and add the broccoli florets. Steam 24 min/Varoma/speed 1, stirring once during cooking to even out the cooking. Then remove the Varoma.
3. Add the pasta to the contents of the bowl, then put the Varoma back in place and add the pears.
4. Then, cook for the time indicated on the packet/98°C/reverse direction/simmer speed. Remove the Varoma, then drain the broccoli and pears. Drain the pasta using the simmering basket.
5. Preheat the oven to 200°C (Th. 6-7).
6. Place butter in mixing bowl then melt 2 min/100°C/speed 1.
7. Add flour and mix 10 sec/speed 3.
8. Add milk, salt, pepper and nutmeg then cook 9 min/90°C/speed 4.
9. Then add the blue cheese and mix 20 sec/speed 5. Transfer to the gratin dish. Sprinkle with grated parmesan, then put in the oven and cook for 10-12 minutes at 200°C.
10. Serve hot.

69. Risotto with gourmet cereals

Ingredients for 4 servings:

- ✓ 40 g parmesan, cut into pieces,
- ✓ 80 g carrot, cut into pieces,
- ✓ 80 g zucchini, cut into pieces,
- ✓ 50 g fresh button mushrooms, halved,
- ✓ 40 g shallots, halved + 20 g of olive oil,
- ✓ 250 g mixed cereal seeds + 40 g of dry white wine,
- ✓ 250g of water + 1 vegetable stock cube,
- ✓ 1 teaspoon of salt, to be adjusted according to taste,

Preparation :

1. Place Parmesan in mixing bowl and grate 10 sec/speed 10. Transfer to a bowl and set aside.
2. Place carrot, zucchini and mushrooms in mixing bowl then grate 5 sec/speed 5. Transfer to a bowl and set aside.
3. Then, place shallots in mixing bowl and chop 5 sec/speed 5. Scrape down sides of mixing bowl with spatula.
4. Add olive oil, then sauté 3 min/120°C/speed 1, without the measuring cup.
5. Add the gourmet cereals and the grated vegetables, then brown 3 min/120°C/reverse/speed 1, without the measuring cup.
6. Then add the white wine and cook 1 min/100°C/reverse/speed 1, without the measuring cup.
7. Add the water, stock cube and salt, then carefully scrape the bottom of the bowl with the spatula to loosen the cereal if necessary. Cook 10 min/90°C/speed 1 (or taking into account the cooking time indicated on the packet), replacing the measuring cup with the simmering basket on the bowl lid to avoid splashes.
8. Let the risotto rest for 1 minute in the bowl, then transfer it to a dish. Using the spatula, add the grated Parmesan then serve immediately.

70. Creole fish ramekins

Ingredients for 6 servings:

- ✓ 600 g of white fish fillets (cod, hake, pollock, etc.), cut into pieces (1 cm),
- ✓ 10 g unsalted butter, for the ramekins,
- ✓ 100 g of coconut milk,
- ✓ 2 cloves garlic,
- ✓ 1 tsp. curry powder,
- ✓ 4 eggs,
- ✓ 1 tsp. cornstarch,
- ✓ 2 pinches of cayenne pepper,
- ✓ 1 of salt, to be adjusted according to taste,
- ✓ 1 of pepper, to be adjusted according to taste,

Preparation :

1. Put the pieces of fish in a hollow container and set aside.

2. Preheat the oven to 200°C (Th. 6-7). Butter 6 ramekins and set aside.

3. Place coconut milk, garlic and curry in mixing bowl then heat 3 min/98°C/speed 1. Pour over fish pieces, cover in cling film and leave to marinate for 5 minutes.

4. Drain the fish using the simmering basket, making sure to reserve the marinade. Divide the fish pieces into the ramekins and set aside.

5. Place eggs, cornstarch, cayenne pepper, salt, pepper and marinade in mixing bowl then mix 20 sec/speed 4. Spread over fish in ramekins. Put in the oven and cook for 15 minutes at 200°C.

6. Serve hot.

71. Pan-fried turkey with vegetables

Ingredients for 4 Servings:

- ✓ 1 onion,
- ✓ 3 cloves,
- ✓ 10g of olive oil,
- ✓ 600g of turkey,
- ✓ Salt and pepper,
- ✓ 2 zucchinis, diced,
- ✓ 1 broccoli,
- ✓ 2 tbsp dried oregano,
- ✓ 1 tsp. dried basil,
- ✓ 400g of tomato sauce,
- ✓ 4 sprigs of coriander,
- ✓ 1 lime,

Preparation :

1. Put the onion cut in half in the bowl of the Thermomix and the garlic then mix 5 sec/speed 5. Scrape down sides of bowl with spatula.
2. Add the olive oil then cook 3min/95°C/speed 1.
3. Add the turkey cut into pieces then distribute the zucchini cut into cubes and the broccoli cut into florets in the bowl then cook 4 min/Varoma/reverse/Speed. Simmering.
4. Add the tomato sauce, salt, pepper, oregano and chopped basil then cook 10min/Varoma/reverse/Speed. Simmering. Extend the cooking if necessary.
5. Transfer the meat and vegetables to a serving dish and sprinkle with chopped coriander and lime wedges.
6. Variation: You can replace the turkey with chicken or beef.
7. Tip: You can accompany this dish with quinoa.

72. Turkey meatballs and vegetable tagliatelle

Ingredients for 4 Servings:

- ✓ 100 g onion, quartered,
- ✓ 500 g turkey fillet, skinless, in large chunks,
- ✓ 100 g of fresh spinach,
- ✓ 1 bunch of fresh coriander, leaves removed,
- ✓ 500g of water,
- ✓ 200 g carrots, in tagliatelle,
- ✓ 200 g zucchini, tagliatelle,
- ✓ 50 g of pine nuts,
- ✓ 250 g Greek yogurt, 0% fat,
- ✓ salt and ground pepper,

Preparation :

1. Prepare the dumplings. Place onion in mixing bowl and chop 5 sec/speed 5. Scrape down sides with spatula.

2. Add turkey, spinach and coriander then mix 10 sec/speed 5. Form 20 meatballs.

3. Place the water in the bowl. Place the meatballs on the steamer tray and the tagliatelle in the Varoma. Install the Varoma assembly. Cook 15 min/Varoma/speed 2.

4. Meanwhile, prepare the sauce. Dry toast the pine nuts in a pan then mix them with the yogurt. Salt, pepper.

5. Serve the meatballs with the vegetable tagliatelle and the pine nut sauce.

73. Gluten-free cauliflower gratin

Ingredients for 4 Servings:

- ✓ 600g of water + 1 tbsp. coarse salt,
- ✓ 1000 g cauliflower, cut into florets,
- ✓ 1 onion,
- ✓ 1 clove of garlic,
- ✓ 50 g Gruyère cheese, cut into pieces,
- ✓ 50 g parmesan, cut into pieces,
- ✓ 20 g unsalted butter, and a little for the dish,
- ✓ 20 g of rice flour,
- ✓ 250g of milk,
- ✓ 1 egg yolk,
- ✓ 1 tbsp. heaped coffee of old-fashioned mustard,
- ✓ A pinch of ground nutmeg,
- ✓ 1 to 2 pinches of salt, to be adjusted according to taste,
- ✓ 1 to 2 pinches of pepper, to be adjusted according to taste,

Preparation :

1. Put the water and coarse salt in the bowl. Position the Varoma, weigh the cauliflower into it then steam 30 min/Varoma/speed 1. Remove the Varoma and set aside. Clean the bowl.
2. Place Gruyère and Parmesan in mixing bowl then grate 8 sec/speed 9. Transfer to a bowl and set aside.
3. Preheat the oven to 180°C (Th. 6). Butter a baking dish and set aside.
4. Place butter, rice flour and milk in mixing bowl then cook 10 min/90°C/speed 3.
5. Add egg yolk, old-fashioned mustard, nutmeg, salt, pepper, onion cut in 4 and garlic clove then mix 8 sec/speed 4.
6. Garnish the prepared dish with cauliflower, drizzle with sauce and sprinkle with grated cheese. Place in the oven and cook for 25 minutes at 180°C, until the surface of the gratin is golden brown. Serve hot.

74. Express vegetarian pizza

Ingredients for 6 Servings:

- ✓ 240g of water,
- ✓ 400 g of wheat flour, and a little for flouring,
- ✓ 30 g extra virgin olive oil, and a little for finishing,
- ✓ 1 teaspoon of baking powder (½ sachet),
- ✓ 1 tsp of salt,
- ✓ 100 g of tomato sauce,
- ✓ 150 g mozzarella, cut into pieces (2-3 cm),
- ✓ 100 g canned artichoke hearts, cut into pieces,
- ✓ 75 g red onion, thinly sliced,
- ✓ dehydrated oregano, for garnish,

Preparation :

1. Place water, flour, olive oil, baking powder and salt in mixing bowl then mix 15 sec/speed 6. Transfer to a floured bowl, cover with cling film and leave to rise for around 20 minutes.

2. Preheat the oven to 250°C (Th. 8-9). Line a baking sheet with baking paper and set aside.

3. On a lightly floured work surface, thinly roll out the dough (5 mm) with a rolling pin into a rectangle the size of the prepared baking sheet, then transfer it onto the latter.

4. Spread the tomato sauce over the dough, then arrange the mozzarella, artichokes and onions. Sprinkle with oregano, drizzle with olive oil, then bake and cook for 15 minutes at 250°C or until the pastry is golden brown.

5. Serve immediately.

75. Cuban Piccadillo

Ingredients for 6 Servings:

- ✓ 80 g onion, halved,
- ✓ 1 clove of garlic + 20 g of olive oil,
- ✓ 200 g red peppers, diced + 3 tbsp. coffee cumin seeds,
- ✓ 100 g of dry white wine + 300 g of tomato sauce,
- ✓ 600 g potatoes, cut into cubes,
- ✓ 500 g minced meat,
- ✓ 2 pinches of ground pepper, to be adjusted according to taste,
- ✓ 60 g of green olives stuffed with peppers,
- ✓ 60 g of raisins,
- ✓ 30 g drained capers in vinegar,

Preparation:

1. Place onion and garlic in mixing bowl then chop 5 sec/speed 5. Scrape down sides of mixing bowl with spatula.
2. Add 10 g olive oil and sauté 5 min/120°C/speed 1, without the measuring cup.
3. Add peppers and 2 tbsp. coffee cumin, then cook 8 min/100°C/reverse/simmer speed.
4. Then add the white wine and tomato sauce, set up the Varoma and add the potatoes, then steam 20 min/Varoma/speed 1. Meanwhile, heat a frying pan over high heat and cook. brown the minced meat, the tbsp. coffee remaining cumin seeds and pepper with the remaining 10 g of olive oil.
5. Remove the Varoma and reserve the potatoes.
6. Add cooked ground meat, green olives, raisins and capers then cook 8 min/100°C/simmer speed. Transfer the cooked potatoes to a dish and mix with the spatula.
7. Adjust the seasoning, if necessary, then serve immediately.
8. Variation: I replaced the potatoes with eggplant.

76. Zucchini veal meatballs and yogurt sauce

Ingredients for 4 Servings:

- ✓ 15 fresh mint leaves,
- ✓ the zest of a lemon, grated,
- ✓ 100 g onion, quartered,
- ✓ 1 clove of garlic,
- ✓ 700 g of minced veal,
- ✓ Salt + ground pepper,
- ✓ 10 sprigs of fresh mint, stripped and chopped,
- ✓ 125 g of Greek yogurt,
- ✓ the juice of a lemon,
- ✓ 4 tbsp. olive oil,
- ✓ 700g zucchini, sliced + 500g of water,

Preparation :

1. In the bowl, place the mint, lemon zest, onion and garlic. Mix 5 sec/speed 5. Scrape down sides with spatula.
2. Add the veal, salt and pepper and mix 10 sec/reverse/speed 2. Form 16 meatballs, then set aside in the fridge. Wash and dry the bowl.
3. Prepare the sauce. Place the leafed and chopped mint, yogurt, lemon juice and olive oil in the bowl. Season with salt and pepper and mix 5 sec/speed 5. Set aside. Rinse and dry the bowl.
4. Place the zucchinis in the Varoma and the water in the mixing bowl then insert the Varoma and cook 10 min/Varoma/speed 1. Meanwhile, in a frying pan, heat the olive oil then brown the meatballs to brown them.
5. Place the meatballs on the steamer tray then insert the tray into the Varoma and continue cooking 10 min/Varoma/speed 1.
6. Serve the meatballs with the zucchinis and the yoghurt sauce.

77. Zucchini beef keftas and pepper sauce

Ingredients for 4 Servings:

- ✓ 250 g of couscous seeds + 250g of hot water,
- ✓ salt and ground pepper + 1 onion, quartered,
- ✓ 4 sprigs of fresh parsley + 500g ground beef, 5% fat,
- ✓ 1 tsp. cumin powder + 4 red bell peppers, diced,
- ✓ 100g onion + 2 tbsp. tablespoon olive oil,
- ✓ 1 tablespoon of ras el-hanout,
- ✓ 2 zucchinis, in 3 mm slices,
- ✓ 500 g of water,
- ✓ A few sprigs of fresh coriander,

Preparation :

1. In a bowl, place the couscous, hot water and a pinch of salt. Let it swell.
2. Prepare the dumplings. Place the onion and parsley in the bowl. Blend 3 sec/speed 5.
3. Add meat, cumin, salt and pepper then mix 10 sec/reverse/speed 4. Transfer to a bowl and rinse the mixing bowl.
4. Prepare the sauce. Mix peppers and onion 5 sec/speed 5. Scrape down sides with spatula.
5. Add the oil, the ras el-hanout and cook 15 min/100°C/speed 2 without the measuring cup. Meanwhile, form 4 cm oval stuffing balls. Place them on the steamer tray and the zucchinis in the Varoma. Fluff the couscous with a fork and distribute it evenly on the steamer tray.
6. Insert the measuring cup and blend the cooked sauce 10 sec/speed 7. Set aside and rinse the bowl.
7. Pour 500 g of water into the bowl and install the Varoma set. Steam 17 min/Varoma/speed 1.
8. Place sauce and meatballs in skillet. Heat for 5 minutes, stirring. Serve with couscous, zucchini and a few sprigs of fresh coriander.

78. Pan-fried beef and green cabbage

Ingredients for 4 Servings:

- ✓ 1 sweet yellow onion,
- ✓ 1 large head of green cabbage,
- ✓ 2 cloves garlic,
- ✓ 10g of olive oil,
- ✓ 600g ground beef,
- ✓ 1 green pepper,
- ✓ 1 red pepper,
- ✓ 400g of tomato sauce,
- ✓ 1 tablespoon smoked paprika,
- ✓ 1 teaspoon dried oregano,
- ✓ 2 tablespoons apple cider vinegar,
- ✓ salt and black pepper,
- ✓ A small handful of chopped fresh parsley or chopped Italian parsley to garnish

Preparation :

1. Place the onion and garlic in the thermomix bowl then mix 5sec/speed 5. Scrape down sides of bowl with spatula.
2. Add ground meat, olive oil and cook 5 min/100°C/reverse/speed 1.
3. Add diced green pepper, diced red pepper, paprika, oregano, salt and pepper then cook 3min/100°C/reverse/speed 1.
4. Then add the cabbage cut into strips, the tomato sauce, the apple cider vinegar then cook 15min/Varoma/reverse/speed 1.
5. When the bell rings, transfer to a serving dish and sprinkle with chopped parsley.

79. Chicken m'charmel and green beans

Ingredients for 4 Servings:

- ✓ 600g of chicken,
- ✓ 4 cloves of garlic,
- ✓ 1 bunch of coriander,
- ✓ Salt,
- ✓ 1 tsp cumin,
- ✓ 1 tsp paprika,
- ✓ 20 g of olive oil,
- ✓ The juice of a lemon,
- ✓ 150g of water,
- ✓ 500g of green beans,

Preparation :

1. Put the garlic and the coriander in the bowl of the thermomix then mix 5 sec/speed 7. Scrape down sides of bowl with spatula.

2. Add salt, cumin, paprika, olive oil and lemon juice then mix 5 sec/speed 3.

3. Cut the chicken into pieces and place on a plate. Brush the chicken with the chermoula and refrigerate for 1 hour.

4. Fit the whisk and insert the marinated chicken. Add the water to the thermomix bowl. Set up the Varoma and insert the stemmed beans and the mushrooms cut into pieces. Cook 30min/Varoma/reverse/speed. Simmering.

5. When the bell rings, remove the Varoma, distribute the vegetables and the chicken with the chermoula in a serving dish.

80. Chicken and leek gratin

Ingredients for 4 Servings:

- ✓ 1 onion,
- ✓ 1 clove of garlic,
- ✓ 10g of olive oil,
- ✓ 500 g of chicken breast,
- ✓ 4 white leeks,
- ✓ 40 g of cornstarch,
- ✓ 60 g grated parmesan,
- ✓ 400 ml of skimmed milk,
- ✓ A little nutmeg,
- ✓ 10g of olive oil,
- ✓ Salt and pepper,

Preparation :

1. Add the onion cut in half and the clove of garlic then mix 5 sec/speed 5. Scrape down sides of bowl with spatula.
2. Add the olive oil and the leeks cut into sections then cook 5 min/90°C/reverse/speed. Simmering.
3. Add the chicken cut into pieces and cook 5 min/110°C/reverse/speed. Simmering.
4. Preheat the oven to 180°C.
5. When the bell rings, transfer the preparation to a gratin dish.
6. Without rinsing the bowl, add the milk, cornstarch, nutmeg, salt and pepper and cook 6min/90°C/speed 2.
7. Transfer to the gratin dish, sprinkle with parmesan and put in the oven for 20 minutes at 180°C.
8. Variation: Replace Parmesan with rolled oats.

81. Rice with tomato and sausages

Ingredients for 4 Servings:

- ✓ 60 g shallots, halved,
- ✓ 10 g of olive oil,
- ✓ 320 g of long grain rice,
- ✓ 500 g tomatoes, peeled and diced,
- ✓ 1 tsp. tomato puree,
- ✓ 500g of water,
- ✓ ½ teaspoon, to be adjusted according to taste,
- ✓ 1 tsp. paprika, to be adjusted according to taste,
- ✓ 2 pinches of cayenne pepper powder, to be adjusted according to taste,
- ✓ 8 chipolata sausages, previously pricked with a fork,

Preparation :

1. Place shallots in mixing bowl and chop 5 sec/speed 5. Scrape down sides of mixing bowl with spatula.

2. Add olive oil and sweat 3 min/120°C/simmer speed.

3. Add rice and sauté 5 min/120°C/reverse/speed 1.

4. Then add the diced tomatoes, tomato paste, water, salt, paprika and chili. Place Varoma in position and add sausages, then steam 16 min/Varoma/reverse/speed 1. Remove Varoma.

5. Cut the sausages into 2 cm sections and brown them in olive oil in a frying pan over high heat.

6. Serve the tomato rice topped with pieces of sausage.

82. Spaghetti squash Bolognese

Ingredients for 4 Servings:

- ✓ 1 large spaghetti squash,
- ✓ 500 g minced beef 5%,
- ✓ 1 onion,
- ✓ 1 clove of garlic,
- ✓ 4 tomatoes,
- ✓ 40cl of tomato coulis,
- ✓ Provencal herbs,
- ✓ 10g of olive oil,
- ✓ Salt,
- ✓ Pepper,

Preparation :

1. Preheat the oven to 180°C.
2. Cut the squash in half (lengthwise), remove the center with the seeds and the stringy part. Place the pieces on a baking sheet lined with baking paper, face down. Bake for 30 minutes then turn the squash, covering it with aluminum foil. Continue cooking for 15 minutes.
3. Meanwhile, put the onion and garlic in the Thermomix bowl and mix 5 sec/speed 5.
4. Add 10g of olive oil and cook 5min/100°C/reverse/speed 1 (without the measuring cup).
5. Add the tomatoes, tomato coulis, minced meat, Provence herbs, salt and pepper and cook 20min/100°C/reverse/speed 1.
6. Once the squash is cooked, let it cool and remove the flesh with a fork to form spaghetti.
7. Add the spaghetti to a serving dish and add the Bolognese sauce. Stir gently and serve.

83. Veal with peppers in hot sauce

Ingredients for 6 Servings:

- 20 g of olive oil,
- 1000 g veal cutlets, cut into strips (1 x 5 cm),
- 1 tablespoon of dried chili flakes, to be adjusted according to taste,
- 50 g of soy sauce,
- 15 g of oyster sauce,
- 50 g of rice wine,
- 400 g bell peppers (green and red) julienned,
- 400g sweet onions, julienned,
- 4 tablespoons toasted sesame oil,

Preparation :

1. Place the oil in the mixing bowl and add the veal strips and brown 10 min/120°C/reverse direction/speed 1.

2. Add the dried chili, soy sauce, oyster sauce and rice wine. Place Varoma in position and add green peppers and onions, then steam 10 min/Varoma/reverse/speed 1. Remove Varoma and set aside.

3. Transfer the contents of the bowl to a wok and cook over high heat until the liquid has reduced almost completely. Add the cooked vegetables and sesame oil to the wok, then mix with the spatula.

4. Serve immediately.

84. Turkey biryani

Ingredients for 4 Servings:

- ✓ 700g sliced turkey cutlets,
- ✓ 1 natural stirred yogurt,
- ✓ 1.5 tbsp. powdered garam masala,
- ✓ 1 pistil of saffron,
- ✓ 200g of milk + 15 g sesame oil,
- ✓ 1 tsp. cinnamon powder,
- ✓ 1 tsp. powdered cumin,
- ✓ 3 cloves + 1 tsp. paprika,
- ✓ 2 pods of cardamom seeds,
- ✓ 110 g onion, cut in 4,
- ✓ 1 clove of garlic + 10 g of fresh ginger,
- ✓ 400 g diced tomato pulp,
- ✓ Salt + ground pepper,

Preparation :

1. Prepare the marinade. Pour the meat into a bowl with the yogurts and the garam masala. Mix, cover and refrigerate for 8 hours.
2. Infuse the saffron in a glass of milk, mix and set aside.
3. Pour oil into mixing bowl and heat 1 min/100°C/speed 1.
4. Add spices and heat 25 sec/100°C/speed 1.
5. Add the onion, garlic and ginger and sauté 5 min/120°C/reverse/speed 1, without the measuring cup.
6. Add tomato pulp and continue cooking 5 min/100°C/reverse/speed 1.
7. Blend 12 sec/speed 4.5, then scrape down sides with spatula.
8. Add the meat and the marinade, season and cook 25 mins/90°C/reverse direction/simmering speed, without the measuring beaker, pouring the saffron milk through the opening after 10 mins of cooking.

85. Wok of prawns with quinoa

Ingredients for 4 Servings:

- ✓ 1 broccoli,
- ✓ 1 cauliflower,
- ✓ 300 g quinoa cooked beforehand,
- ✓ 400 g peeled prawns,
- ✓ 1 tablespoon of olive oil,
- ✓ 800 g of water,
- ✓ 1 tablespoon of sesame seeds,
- ✓ 1 teaspoon of powdered ginger,

Preparation :

1. Cut the broccoli and the cauliflower. Put them in a bouquet in the Varoma. Put 800g of water in the bowl and cook 30min/Varoma/Vit. 1.

2. Meanwhile, in a sauté pan or wok, heat the olive oil and add the prawns and brown them.

3. Once the vegetables are cooked, add them to the wok with the shrimp. Add cooked quinoa.

4. Mix everything and add sesame seeds and ginger powder.

5. Serve immediately hot.

86. Quinotto with seitan mushrooms and parmesan cheese

Ingredients for 4 Servings:

- ✓ 80 g parmesan, cut into pieces,
- ✓ 100 g onion, in pieces,
- ✓ 10g of olive oil,
- ✓ 300g fresh button mushrooms, sliced,
- ✓ 100 g red bell pepper, diced,
- ✓ 250 g of quinoa,
- ✓ 400g of water,
- ✓ Salt + ground pepper,
- ✓ 200 g seitan, in 1 cm thick strips,
- ✓ 5 sprigs of fresh parsley, stripped and chopped,

Preparation :

1. Mix parmesan 8 sec/speed 5. Set aside.
2. In bowl, place onion and chop 5 sec/speed 5. Scrape down sides of bowl with spatula.
3. Add olive oil, mushrooms and bell pepper. Brown 5 min/120°C/reverse/simmer speed.
4. Add the quinoa, then the 400 g of water. Salt and pepper. Cook 14 min/100°C/reverse/simmer speed.
5. When the bell rings, add the seitan strips and continue cooking 3 min/100°C/reverse/simmer speed.
6. Serve with parmesan and chopped parsley.
7. Variation: You can replace the seitan with diced tofu.

87. Fish sausages with spinach and vegetables

Ingredients for 4 Servings:

- ✓ 1 clove of garlic, peeled and degermed,
- ✓ 2 shallots + 10 g of olive oil,
- ✓ 200 g of fresh baby spinach,
- ✓ 300 g boneless white fish fillets, cut into 3 cm pieces (cod, saithe, whiting, etc.),
- ✓ 2 egg whites + 40g of milk + Salt + ground pepper,
- ✓ 800g of water + 300g broccoli, in florets,
- ✓ 200 g of fresh green beans,

Preparation :

1. Place garlic and shallots in mixing bowl, chop 3 sec/speed 8. Scrape down sides of mixing bowl with spatula.
2. Add olive oil and spinach, cook 5 min/98°C/speed 3. Reserve spinach in a bowl. Rinse the bowl.
3. Place fish in mixing bowl, chop 8 sec/speed 4. Scrape down sides.
4. Add egg whites, mix 5 sec/speed 4. Scrape down sides.
5. Add 20 g milk, salt and pepper then mix 10 sec/speed 5.
6. Cut four rectangles of heatproof cling film. Spread the fish stuffing on it. Place the chopped spinach in the center, then roll gently to obtain sausages. Tie the ends. Rinse the bowl.
7. Pour the water into the bowl. Place the fish sausages in the Varoma, arrange the broccoli and the beans on the steam tray, salt and pepper them. Put the Varoma set in place, cook 17 min/Varoma/speed 2. Remove the Varoma set.
8. Pour 1 small ladle of cooking water into a sauce boat, salt and pepper, pour in the remaining 20 g of milk then mix. Remove the cling film from the sausages, cut them into slices and serve them with the vegetables and the sauce.

88. Swordfish on papillote

Ingredients for 2 people:

- ✓ 1 fillet of swordfish,
- ✓ 2 slices of lemon,
- ✓ 1 drizzle of olive oil for the foil,
- ✓ salt to taste,
- ✓ 75 g of extra virgin olive oil,
- ✓ 1/2 clove of garlic,
- ✓ 500 g of crushed tomato,
- ✓ 1/2 teaspoon of sugar,
- ✓ 75 g of white breadcrumbs (from the day before),

A little vinegar,

Preparation :

1. Start by putting the crushed tomatoes, sugar and peeled garlic in the bowl of your Thermomix, then set to speed 5 for 30 seconds.
2. Add the breadcrumbs and the vinegar and program at speed 5 for 30 seconds, then set at speed 10 for 2 minutes.
3. Scrape the sides with a spatula, then program at speed 5 for 1 minute and pour the oil through the hole in the lid.
4. Transfer the salmorejo to a bowl and set aside in the refrigerator.
5. Wash the bowl of the thermomix and pour 300 g of water into it.
6. Put the swordfish steak in a rectangle of parchment paper, then season, pour a drizzle of olive oil and place two slices of lemon on top.
7. Then, wrap the swordfish steak in the parchment paper, then put in the Varoma and place on the bowl of the thermomix.
8. Program at speed 2 for 15 minutes at Varoma temperature.
9. At the buzzer, remove the swordfish from the Varoma and cut into slices.
10. Serve the salmorejo in deep plates or bowls and put the slices of swordfish on top, then drizzle with olive oil.

89. Pollock dumplings in Thai broth

Ingredients for 4 Servings:

- ✓ 600 g skinless saithe fillets, in pieces,
- ✓ 2 shallots, in pieces,
- ✓ 1 tablespoon sweet chili sauce,
- ✓ 4 tablespoons of fish sauce (nuoc-mâm),
- ✓ 30 g of cornstarch,
- ✓ 1 bunch of fresh coriander, stemmed,
- ✓ 1000 g of water,
- ✓ 1 vegetable stock cube,
- ✓ 2 carrots, in tagliatelle,
- ✓ 2 leeks, minced,
- ✓ 100 g of konjac noodles,
- ✓ 3/4 limes (1/2 squeezed lemon(s) and 2 cut into quarters),

Preparation :

1. Prepare the dumplings. Place the fish in the bowl with the shallot, sweet chili sauce, nuoc-mâm, cornstarch and ½ bunch of coriander. Mix 20 sec/speed 6 to obtain a homogeneous filling. Transfer the stuffing to a salad bowl and set aside. Rinse and dry the bowl. Form the balls the size of a small ping-pong ball and place them on the steamer tray. Insert the steamer tray into the Varoma and set aside.
2. Prepare the broth. Pour the water into the bowl with the stock cube and heat 10 min/100°C/reverse direction/speed 1.
3. Add the carrots and leeks to the bowl, install the Varoma set and cook 14 min/100°C/reverse/simmer speed. Remove the Varoma assembly. (Meanwhile fry the LIV Happy noodles with konjac in a pan).
4. Add the noodles, the juice of 1 lime and the nuoc-mâm to the broth, put the Varoma set back in place and simmer for about 5 min/100°C/reverse/simmer speed.
5. Just before serving, add the rest of the coriander and enjoy hot with lemon wedges to squeeze at the last moment.

90. Tomato crumble

Ingredients for 4 Servings:

- ✓ 8 tomatoes,
- ✓ 2 white onions,
- ✓ 3 cloves of garlic,
- ✓ 10g of olive oil,
- ✓ 60g rolled oats,
- ✓ 50g of grated parmesan,
- ✓ Tabasco,
- ✓ 1 tbsp Herbes de Provence,
- ✓ 1 tsp thyme/oregano,
- ✓ Salt and pepper,

Preparation :

1. Preheat the oven to 180°C.
2. Cut the tomatoes into slices and arrange them in a gratin dish. Sprinkle with a drizzle of olive oil, salt and pepper and put in the oven for 45 minutes.
3. Meanwhile, add the halved onions and the garlic cloves to the thermomix bowl then mix 5sec/speed 5. Scrape down sides of bowl with spatula.
4. Add olive oil and cook 5min/90°C/reverse/speed. Simmering. Leave to cool in the bowl.
5. Then add the oat flakes, parmesan, tabasco, Provence herbs, thyme, salt and pepper and mix 20sec/reverse/speed 2.
6. Take the dish out of the oven and drain the juice from the tomatoes.
7. Add the crumble to the tomatoes and put in the oven for 30 minutes at 160°C.
8. Serve warm or cold.
9. Variation: Replace oats with breadcrumbs.

91. Pasta clafoutis

Ingredients for 6 Servings:

- ✓ 1500 g of water,
- ✓ 1 whole egg + 2 yolks,
- ✓ 250 g of milk,
- ✓ 10 g of cornstarch,
- ✓ 2 pansies of nutmeg,
- ✓ Salt,
- ✓ Pepper,
- ✓ 30 g of breadcrumbs,
- ✓ 150 g of raw pasta,
- ✓ 200 g of smoked matches of lardons or bacon,
- ✓ 200 g sliced Paris mushrooms,
- ✓ 70 g grated Comté,

Preparation :

1. Add water and cook 10 min/Varoma/speed 1.
2. Add the pasta and cook for the cooking time indicated on the package/100°/Simmer speed/reverse knife. Without the cup.
3. When the bell rings pass the pasta through a colander then set aside.
4. Put the whole egg, the yolks, the cornstarch, the milk, the nutmeg, the salt and the pepper in the bowl then mix 30 sec/speed 4.
5. Sprinkle the bottom of a silicone or previously buttered dish with half the breadcrumbs.
6. Place half of the cooked pasta, half of the matchsticks, half of the mushrooms then half of the grated Comté cheese.
7. Pour in half of the egg mixture.
8. Repeat with a layer of pasta, then matchsticks, mushrooms and the rest of the mixture.
9. Sprinkle with gruyere, salt and pepper and finish with the rest of the breadcrumbs.
10. Put in the oven for 40 minutes at 180°C.

92. Butternut squash stuffed with chicken

Ingredients for 4 Servings:

- ✓ 1 butternut squash,
- ✓ 800g of water,
- ✓ 120 g rice, red,
- ✓ 2 shallots,
- ✓ 100 g of fresh spinach, and 4 handfuls for serving,
- ✓ 2 tablespoons of olive oil,
- ✓ 1 tablespoon of spice mix,
- ✓ 160g chicken, diced,

Preparation :

1. Cut the squash in half lengthwise. Remove the seeds. Pour the water into the bowl and put the rice into the simmering basket.
2. Rinse it out and install the simmering basket. Place the 2 squash halves in the Varoma, insert the Varoma and cook 35 min/Varoma/speed 1. Set the rice and squash aside and empty the bowl.
3. Preheat the oven to 180°C.
4. Using a knife, hollow out the inside of the squash halves, taking care to leave 1 cm of flesh all around the skin. Dice the flesh.
5. Place shallots and 100 g spinach leaves in mixing bowl then chop 5 sec/speed 5.
6. Add oil and spices and sauté 3 min/120°C/speed 2.
7. Add chicken and continue cooking 5 min/120°C/reverse/speed 2.
8. Then add the diced squash and the drained rice and continue cooking 5 min/80°C/reverse/speed 1. Fill the squash with the stuffing.
9. Place the squash on a baking sheet and roast for 20 minutes at 180°C.

93. Cauliflower and leek gratin Tartiflette style

Ingredients for 4 Servings:

- ✓ 600g of water,
- ✓ 1 cauliflower,
- ✓ 4 leeks,
- ✓ 100g of onions,
- ✓ 1 clove of garlic,
- ✓ 10g of olive oil,
- ✓ 200g of bacon matches,
- ✓ 80g of rice cream,
- ✓ 2 pinches of nutmeg,
- ✓ Salt and pepper,
- ✓ 1/2 reblochon,

Preparation :

1. Put the water in the thermomix bowl and set up the Varoma. Put the cauliflower cut into florets and the leeks cut into small sections in the Varoma. Steam 20min/Varoma/Vit.1. Remove the Varoma and transfer to a gratin dish then set aside.
2. Preheat the oven to 180°C.
3. Put the onion in the Thermomix bowl, add the garlic clove and mix 5 sec/speed 5. Scrape down sides of bowl with spatula.
4. Add the olive oil and the matches then cook 5 min/100°C/reverse/speed. 1.
5. Add cream, nutmeg, salt and pepper then stir 30sec/reverse/speed 3. Transfer to the gratin dish. Cut a reblochon into strips and place it on top of the dish.
6. Put in the oven for 30 minutes at 180°C, monitoring the coloring.
7. Serve hot, accompanied for example by a green salad.
8. Variation: For a lighter recipe, replace the reblochon by sprinkling your gratin with oatmeal.

94. Filet mignon with prunes and vegetables

Ingredients for 6 Servings:

- ✓ 500 g pork tenderloin,
- ✓ Salt + ground pepper,
- ✓ 6 slices of bacon,
- ✓ 80 g pitted prunes,
- ✓ 1000g water,
- ✓ 200 g carrots, sliced,
- ✓ 200 g pumpkin cut into cubes,
- ✓ 120 g zucchini, diced,
- ✓ 1 red onion, minced,
- ✓ A few sprigs of fresh chives, chopped,

Preparation :

1. Split the filet mignon in half lengthwise, without cutting it completely.

2. Salt and pepper the bacon, then place it and the prunes in the center of the filet mignon. Close it by tying it like a roast with kitchen twine. Place it in the Varoma.

3. Pour the water into the bowl, install the Varoma and steam 35 min/Varoma/speed 1.

4. Remove the Varoma and transfer the roast to the steamer tray. Place the vegetables in the Varoma and insert the steam tray, then continue cooking 15 min/Varoma/speed 1.

5. Serve the sliced roast with the vegetable tagliatelle, red onion and sprinkle with chives.

95. Meatballs with prune sauce

Ingredients for 4 persons :

- ✓ 12 meatballs of pork or beef,
- ✓ 40 g of extra virgin olive oil,
- ✓ 1 clove of garlic,
- ✓ 220 g onion, cut into quarters,
- ✓ 85 g pitted prunes,
- ✓ 40 g of white wine,
- ✓ 450g chicken, poultry stock or water,
- ✓ salt,

Preparation :

1. Start by peeling the garlic and the onion, then cut them into quarters and put them in the bowl of your thermomix.
2. Add the plums and program at speed 1 for 8 minutes at 120°C.
3. Pour in the wine and set at speed 1 for 5 minutes at Varoma temperature.
4. Next, add the broth and salt, then place the Varoma on the lid with the dumplings inside.
5. Program at speed 1 for 30 minutes at Varoma temperature.
6. Remove the Varoma and blend the sauce at progressive speed 5-7-9 for 20 seconds.
7. Serve your meatballs with the prune sauce and accompany them with rice or salad.
8. Treat yourself.

96. Clafoutis of green asparagus with prawns

Ingredients for 6 Servings:

- ✓ 800g of water,
- ✓ 1 bunch (500 g) green asparagus,
- ✓ 500 g of cooked prawns,
- ✓ 1 clove of garlic,
- ✓ 5 sprigs of parsley,
- ✓ 2 eggs,
- ✓ 180g of milk,
- ✓ Salt,
- ✓ Pepper,

Preparation :

1. Cut the base of the asparagus then pour the 2 or 3 pieces. Arrange them in the Varoma. Fill the bowl with 800 grams of water, put the Varoma in place then program 20min/Varoma/Vit.1.
2. During this time, shell the prawns and incise the "back" to remove the black gut that is there. To book.
3. Preheat the oven to 175°.
4. When the bell rings, remove the Varoma and empty the bowl.
5. Add the garlic clove and the parsley then mix 5 sec/speed 5 Scrape down the sides of the bowl using the spatula.
6. Add eggs, milk, salt and pepper then mix 10 sec/speed 4.
7. Spread the asparagus in a baking dish and add the prawns. Add the device on top.
8. Put in the oven for 25 minutes at 180°C.
9. Tip: You can optionally sprinkle your clafoutis with grated parmesan before baking.

97. Broccoli Walnut and Ricotta Lasagna

Ingredients for 4 persons :

- ✓ 100 g york ham + 300 g of broccoli in small bouquets (without the stem),
- ✓ 100g onion + 2 cloves garlic + 30 g of olive oil,
- ✓ 400 g liquid cream for cooking + 250 g of ricotta cheese,
- ✓ 70 g of grated parmesan + 50 g of crushed walnuts,
- ✓ 18 pre-cooked lasagne sheets + 100 g grated mozzarella cheese,
- ✓ Salt and ground black pepper,

Preparation :

1. Start by preheating the oven to 180°C.
2. Put in the bowl of your thermomix 250 g of water, then place the broccoli in the Varoma and place it on the thermomix.
3. Set to speed 1 for 10 minutes at Varoma temperature, then set the broccoli aside and empty the water from the bowl.
4. Peel the garlic and the onion, then put them in the bowl of the thermomix and set to speed 5 for 3 seconds.
5. Scrape the sides with a spatula, then set at speed 1 for 5 minutes at 120°C.
6. Add the liquid cream, ricotta, grated parmesan, walnuts, salt and pepper, then turn to speed 3 in reverse for 10 seconds.
7. Pour 5 or 6 tablespoons of the cream mixture into a rectangular baking dish of about 20×30 cm.
8. Place 6 lasagna sheets, then pour 1/3 of the cream mixture.
9. Then, distribute half of the broccoli, crumbling it with your fingers, then the chopped ham. Cover with 6 more lasagne sheets and cover with half of the cream mixture, then spread the rest of the broccoli, crumble it and the chopped ham on top.
10. Cover again with the remaining 6 lasagne sheets, then pour in the remaining cream mixture and sprinkle with shredded mozzarella.
11. Bake for 15 to 20 minutes, then brown for another 5 minutes on a grill.
12. Once cooked, let stand for 2 to 3 minutes before serving.
13. Serve and enjoy.

98. Pasta salad with pepper pesto

Ingredients for 4 Servings:

- ✓ 60 g parmesan, cut into pieces,
- ✓ 10 leaves of fresh basil,
- ✓ 50 g of pine nuts,
- ✓ 1 clove of garlic,
- ✓ 100 g roasted red pepper, canned,
- ✓ 50 g of olive oil,
- ✓ 1500g of water,
- ✓ 10 g of coarse salt,
- ✓ 320 g dry pasta, farfalle type,
- ✓ 150 g cherry tomatoes, halved,
- ✓ 50 g olives, cut into rings (optional),

Preparation :

1. Place parmesan in mixing bowl and grate 5 sec/speed. 10. Transfer to a container and set aside.
2. Place basil, pine nuts and garlic in mixing bowl then chop 5 sec/Speed. 5. Scrape down sides of bowl with spatula.
3. Add bell pepper, olive oil and grated parmesan then chop 10 sec/speed. 4. Transfer to an airtight jar and set aside.
4. Place water and salt in mixing bowl then heat 10 min/100°C/speed. 1.
5. Add the pasta and cook the time indicated on the packet/100°C/reverse/speed. 1, without the measuring cup. Drain the pasta using the Varoma and transfer it to a salad bowl. Add the cherry tomatoes, season with pepper pesto, then mix.
6. Keep in the fridge until it's time to serve.

99. Chicken gratin with millet carrots and parmesan cheese

Ingredients for 6 Servings:

- ✓ 100 g parmesan, cut into pieces,
- ✓ 1000g of water,
- ✓ 200 g grain millet,
- ✓ 400 g carrots, cut into pieces,
- ✓ 1 cooked chicken (smoked – approx. 800 g (approx. 400 g of meat)),
- ✓ 100g of milk,
- ✓ 2 eggs,
- ✓ ½ teaspoon, to be adjusted according to taste,
- ✓ 3 pinches of colombo spices, to be adjusted according to taste,

Preparation :

1. Place parmesan in mixing bowl and grate 5 sec/speed 10. Transfer to a bowl and set aside.
2. Preheat the oven to 180°C (Th. 6).
3. Put the water in the bowl. Insert simmering basket and add millet. Place the Varoma in place and add the carrots, then steam 20 min/Varoma/speed 4. Meanwhile, scoop out the chicken flesh and crumble into a large gratin dish, then set aside. Remove Varoma and simmering basket. Empty the bowl.
4. Place the cooked carrots, half of the grated parmesan, milk, eggs, salt and colombo spices in the mixing bowl then blend 30 sec/speed 10.
5. Add cooked millet and mix 20 sec/reverse/speed 3.5. Pour over the chicken in the gratin dish and mix with the spatula. Sprinkle with the remaining grated parmesan, then bake and brown for 20 minutes at 180°C.
6. Serve hot.

100. Cod with coconut-mint sauce and quinoa with onions

Ingredients for 4 Servings:

- ✓ 4 fresh onions, in pieces (green and white),
- ✓ 1 tablespoon of hydrogenated coconut oil,
- ✓ ½ bunch of fresh mint, leafless,
- ✓ 300 g of coconut milk,
- ✓ Salt + ground pepper,
- ✓ 800g of water,
- ✓ 200 g of quinoa, previously rinsed with clear water,
- ✓ 800g zucchini, sliced,
- ✓ 600g cod back, in large cubes,

Preparation :

1. Place spring onions in mixing bowl and chop 5 sec/speed 5.
2. Reserve ¾ of the blended onions in a small bowl, then add the coconut oil to the bowl. Sauté 3 min/100°C/speed 1.
3. Add mint and coconut milk, season with salt and pepper and simmer 10 min/90°C/speed 1. Keep warm.
4. In the unwashed bowl, pour the water. Rinse the quinoa under clear water, then pour it into the bowl with the ¾ reserved onions. Place the zucchini in the Varoma, place the fish cubes on the tray, salt and pepper. Install Varoma set, then cook 20 min/Varoma/speed 1.
5. Serve the fish with the zucchini, quinoa with onions and coconut-mint sauce.

Desserts

101. Blackberry jam

Ingredients for 8 people:

- ✓ 800 g of fresh blackberries,
- ✓ 560 g sugar for jam with added pectin,
- ✓ 2 tbsp. lemon juice,

Preparation :

1. Start by washing the blackberries well, then drain them and put them in the bowl of your thermomix.

2. Add the lemon juice to the bowl, then turn to speed 5 for 5 seconds.

3. Scrape the sides with a spatula, then program at speed 2 for 5 minutes at Varoma temperature, keeping the measuring cup on the lid.

4. Add the sugar and program at speed 2 for 15 minutes at 100°C, placing the simmering basket on top instead of the beaker to avoid splashing.

5. Pour your jam into sterilized jars and close them, then turn them upside down for a few minutes.

6. Then turn the jars right side up and let them cool completely before eating.

7. You can store your jam in the refrigerator.

8. Treat yourself.

102. Mirabelle plum jam

Ingredients for 4 persons :

- ✓ 580 g mirabelle plums,

- ✓ 170 g of crystal sugar,

- ✓ 1 tablespoon of lemon juice,

Preparation :

1. Start by washing the Mirabelle plums, then cut them in half and pit them.

2. Put the Mirabelle plums, crystal sugar and lemon juice in the bowl of your Thermomix.

3. Program at speed 4 for 4 seconds.

4. Scrape the sides with a spatula, then set at speed 1 for 33 minutes at Varoma temperature, placing the basket on the lid.

5. Sterilize your jam jars in boiling water.

6. Divide the jam into the jars and let cool before closing.

7. Treat yourself.

103. Tomato jam

Ingredients for 8 people:

- ✓ 350 g of tomatoes,
- ✓ 125 g special jam sugar,
- ✓ 1 cinnamon stick,
- ✓ 2 cloves,
- ✓ A pinch of ground nutmeg,

Preparation :

1. Start by washing and peeling the tomatoes, then cut them into quarters, removing the stem.

2. Put the tomato quarters as well as the sugar, cinnamon stick, cloves and a pinch of nutmeg in the bowl of your Thermomix.

3. Program at speed 2 for 35 minutes at 100°C, putting the basket in place of the measuring cup.

4. Next, remove the cloves and the cinnamon stick, then turn to speed 4 for a few seconds until the desired consistency is obtained.

5. Pour the jam into a jar and let cool to room temperature, then seal the jar and store in the fridge.

6. If you produce a large quantity, you can put the jam under vacuum in glass jars to be able to enjoy it the rest of the year.

7. Treat yourself.

104. Nougat with pistachios almonds and blueberries

Ingredients for 10 people:

- ✓ 15 g of egg white,
- ✓ 90 g of honey,
- ✓ 80 g of sugar,
- ✓ A pinch of vanilla essence,
- ✓ 60 g unsalted peeled pistachios,
- ✓ 50 g of blueberries,
- ✓ 40 g toasted almonds,
- ✓ 5 g of water,

Preparation :

1. Start by inserting the butterfly into the thermomix bowl, then add the egg whites and set to speed 3 for 15 seconds.
2. Add the honey, sugar, water and vanilla essence, then set to speed 2 for 40 minutes at 100°C without measuring cup.
3. Meanwhile, lightly grease a nougat mold with a little sunflower oil.
4. Remove the butterfly and add the almonds, pistachios and blueberries, then turn to speed 2 in reverse for 10 seconds.
5. Immediately pour the contents of the bowl into the mold and leave to cool for 12 hours.
6. Serve and enjoy.

105. Japanese Dorayakis

Ingredients for 10 double portions:

- ✓ 3 medium eggs,
- ✓ 90-100 g of white sugar,
- ✓ 15 g of honey or maple syrup,
- ✓ 1 teaspoon of sweet wine,
- ✓ 80 ml of water,
- ✓ 1 teaspoon baking soda,
- ✓ 180 g of wheat flour,
- ✓ Nutella,

Preparation :

1. Start by inserting the butterfly in the bowl of the thermomix and put the sugar and the eggs in it.
2. Program at speed 3.5 for 5 minutes.
3. Add the honey and sweet wine, then set to speed 3.5 for 10 seconds.
4. Dissolve the baking soda in 50 ml of water, then pour into the bowl of the thermomix and set to speed 2 for 10 seconds.
5. Remove the butterfly and add the flour, then set to speed 3 for 15 seconds. Transfer the resulting dough to a bowl and leave to rest for 30 minutes.
6. When the paste is ready to use, add 30 ml of water and mix with a spoon.
7. Heat a non-stick pan over high heat, then pour in a tablespoon of batter.
8. When bubbles start to appear, turn it over with a spatula and finish cooking. Do the same with the rest of the dough.
9. Spread Nutella on one pancake and cover it with a second one.
10. Serve and enjoy.

106. Apple and cinnamon ice cream

Ingredients for 2 people:

- ✓ 2 bananas, sliced and frozen,
- ✓ 80 g of apple cream or apple butter,
- ✓ 1 tablespoon (dessert size) ground cinnamon,
- ✓ 1 tablespoon of vanilla paste,

Preparation :

1. Start by putting all the ingredients in the bowl of your thermomix.

2. Program at progressive speed 5-7 for 5 seconds.

3. Scrape the sides with a spatula, then set at speed 5 for 1 minute.

4. Divide between two bowls and serve immediately.

5. Treat yourself.

107. Red liquor ice cream

Ingredients for 8 people:

- ✓ 80 g of red licorice,
- ✓ 280 g of milk,
- ✓ 100 g of white sugar,
- ✓ 40 g of invert sugar,
- ✓ 350 g very cold whipping cream,
- ✓ A few drops of red food coloring,

Preparation :

1. Start by putting the red licorice in the bowl of your Thermomix, then set to progressive speed 5-7-9 for 15 seconds. Scrape the sides with a spatula.
2. Add the milk, sugar and inverted sugar, and then set to speed 1 for 5 minutes at 90°C. Remove from bowl and set aside until mixture is at room temperature.
3. As soon as the mixture has cooled, return it to the bowl and insert the butterfly, then set to speed 3.5 until it is whipped.
4. Add a few drops of red food coloring and stir well.
5. Then, program at speed 2 and pour the cream little by little through the hole in the lid until it is finished.
6. Pour the contents of the bowl into a metal container and place in the freezer for 30 minutes.
7. Take the container out of the freezer and stir with a spoon to break up the ice crystals.
8. Repeat the operation 2 more times, then leave to freeze for at least 2 hours.
9. Serve and enjoy.

108. Pistachio Nutella

Ingredients for 2 jars:

- ✓ 100 g shelled and unsalted pistachios,
- ✓ 100 g of white chocolate,
- ✓ 50 g of butter,
- ✓ 100 g of whole milk,
- ✓ 50 g of sweetened condensed milk,

Preparation :

1. Start by putting the pistachios in the bowl of your thermomix, then set to Turbo mode for 30 seconds.

2. Add the white chocolate cut into pieces, then program at speed 8 for 20 seconds.

3. Scrape the walls with a spatula, then add the whole milk, the condensed milk and the butter.

4. Program at speed 3 for 7 minutes at 50°C.

5. Pour into glass jars and let cool before sealing.

6. Store in the refrigerator.

109. Mini Light Chocolate Cheesecake

Ingredients for 6 people:

- ✓ 85 g dark chocolate, 70% cocoa, chopped,
- ✓ 220 g reduced-fat cream cheese at room temperature,
- ✓ 1 teaspoon of pure vanilla extract,
- ✓ Avocado oil spray for liners,
- ✓ 1 teaspoon of stevia,
- ✓ 1 large egg at room temperature,

Preparation :

1. Start by preheating the oven to 150°C, then line a muffin tin with 6 aluminum cups, not paper.
2. Lightly spray the liners with an avocado oil spray, then set aside.
3. Place the chocolate in a small bowl, then microwave for 30 second sessions, stirring after each session, until the chocolate is melted. Reserve aside.
4. Put the cream cheese, vanilla and stevia in a medium bowl and beat with an electric mixer on the lowest speed for about 30 seconds until smooth. smooth consistency.
5. Next add the melted chocolate and beat until combined, then add the egg and mix until just incorporated (do not over mix).
6. Using a spatula, mix one last time to make sure everything is well incorporated.
7. Pour the batter into the muffin tins, then smooth the top.
8. Bake for about 15 minutes at 150°C, then once the cooking is finished, place the muffin tin on a wire rack and let cool completely.
9. Serve and enjoy.

110. Light candied prunes

Ingredients for 4 persons :

- ✓ 20 pitted prunes (160 grams),
- ✓ 1.5 cups of water,
- ✓ ½ teaspoon of vanilla extract,
- ✓ ¼ teaspoon ground cinnamon,

Preparation :

1. Start by putting the prunes in a small saucepan.

2. Add the water, vanilla and cinnamon, then stir.

3. Bring to a boil, then stir gently and reduce the heat to medium-low.

4. Cover and simmer for 15 minutes until the prunes are tender and bathed in syrup.

5. Transfer the contents of the pan to a heatproof glass container, then let cool at room temperature for about 15 minutes.

6. Then, cover the container and refrigerate for at least 1 hour; this allows the syrup to thicken and the flavors to develop.

7. Serve alone or layer over plain Greek yogurt.

8. Treat yourself.

111. Light Peanut Butter Cup

Ingredients for 6 people:

- ✓ 170 g Lindt 90% Cacao Chocolate, broken into pieces (16 squares),
- ✓ 1 tablespoon of avocado oil + ½ teaspoon of stevia,
- ✓ 4 tablespoons creamy peanut butter spread (not natural peanut butter),
- ✓ 1 tablespoon of coconut flour,

Preparation :

1. Start by lining a 6-cavity muffin pan with paper cups.
2. Place half of the chocolate in a small microwave-safe bowl, then the other half in another small microwave-safe bowl.
3. Place the peanut butter in a third small microwave-safe bowl.
4. Microwave the first small bowl with the chocolate in a 20 second session, stirring after each session, until the chocolate is melted.
5. Then, add 1/2 tablespoon of avocado oil and 1/2 teaspoon of stevia to the melted chocolate.
6. Place a tablespoon of the chocolate mixture in the bottom of each paper cup, spreading it out. Freeze for 5 minutes.
7. Microwave the peanut butter for 20 seconds to soften it, then stir in the coconut flour.
8. Take the muffin pan out of the freezer and place a tablespoon of the peanut butter mixture over the chocolate layer, spreading it with the back of a spoon, not reaching the edges.
9. Place in the freezer for 5 minutes to set.
10. Meanwhile, microwave the first small bowl with the chocolate in a 20 second session, stirring after each session, until the chocolate is melted.
11. Then, add 1/2 tablespoon of avocado oil and 1/2 teaspoon of stevia to the melted chocolate.
12. Once the pan is out of the freezer, place about a tablespoon of the chocolate mixture over the peanut butter layer, spreading it quickly over the bowls and sides.
13. Finally, freeze for 30 to 40 minutes to harden. Then, take off the paper cases and let soften for 5 minutes before tasting.
14. Serve and enjoy. Store peanut butter cups in the refrigerator, in an airtight container, for up to one week.

112. Crumb'cake with hazelnut banana and chocolate

Ingredients for 8 Servings:

The cake:
- ✓ 3 very ripe bananas,
- ✓ 3 eggs,
- ✓ 50 g hazelnut powder,
- ✓ 130 g semi-whole wheat flour T80 (or classic),
- ✓ 1/2 teaspoon baking powder,
- ✓ 80 g of dark chocolate chips,

The crumble:
- ✓ 60 g of agave or coconut blossom syrup,
- ✓ 45 g hazelnut powder,
- ✓ 45 g of wheat flour T80 (or classic),
- ✓ 15 g of hazelnut oil,
- ✓ 1 pinch of ground cinnamon,
- ✓ 1 pinch of salt,

Preparation :

1. Preheat the oven to 180°C.
2. Put the bananas in the bowl of the thermomix, add the eggs then mix 30sec/speed 3.
3. Add the hazelnut powder, flour and baking powder then mix 30 sec/speed 3 (the dough must be homogeneous).
4. Add the chocolate chips and mix 30sec/reverse/Vit.3.
5. Transfer the preparation into a silicone cake mold (or previously buttered).
6. Put the hazelnut powder in the bowl of the thermomix, the flour, the cinnamon, the salt and the hazelnut oil then mix 30sec/speed 3.
7. Add the syrup then mix 30 sec/speed 3 (until a sandy texture is obtained).
8. Transfer the crumble to the cake batter.
9. Put in the oven for 40min at 180°C.

113. Clafoutis coconut mango and banana

Ingredients for 6 Servings:

- ✓ 75 g of flour,
- ✓ 3 eggs,
- ✓ 85 + 15 g grated coconut,
- ✓ 300 g of coconut milk,
- ✓ 1 mango,
- ✓ 2 bananas,

Preparation :

1. Preheat the oven to 175°C.

2. Put the flour, the eggs and the coconut in the bowl of the Thermomix then mix 30sec/Vit.3. Scrape down sides of bowl with spatula.

3. Put the mango cut into pieces in a gratin dish and the bananas cut into slices.

4. When the bell rings, pour the mixture over the fruit.

5. Put in the oven for 35 minutes at 175°C.

6. Sprinkle with the remaining 15g grated coconut.

7. Serve warm or cold.

114. Light Strawberry Orange Dip

Ingredients for 4 persons :

- ✓ 220 g softened cream cheese,

- ✓ 1/4 cup powdered sugar

- ✓ 1/2 teaspoon grated orange zest

- ✓ 30 g chopped strawberries

- ✓ Assortment of fruits of your choice,

Preparation:

1. Start by putting the cream cheese, powdered sugar and orange zest in a small bowl.

2. Beat everything with an electric mixer on low speed until smooth.

3. Then add the strawberries.

4. Place in the fridge until ready to eat.

5. Serve with assorted fruit and enjoy.

115. Chocolate-hazelnut tart

Ingredients for 6 Servings:

- ✓ 125 g of flour,
- ✓ 15 g ground hazelnuts,
- ✓ 45 g of icing sugar,
- ✓ 50 g soft butter, in pieces,
- ✓ 1 egg yolk,
- ✓ 125 g dark chocolate, in pieces,
- ✓ 100 g milk chocolate, in pieces,
- ✓ 150 g of 30-40% fat liquid cream,
- ✓ 50 g of hazelnuts,
- ✓ 1 tbsp sugar,

Preparation :

1. Prepare the pie crust. In the bowl, place the flour, ground hazelnuts, icing sugar, butter and egg yolk. Mix 30 sec/speed. 5. Take the dough out of the bowl, form a ball, wrap it in cling film and place it in the fridge for 2 hours.
2. Roll out the dough with the rolling pin on parchment paper and line the pie dish (Ø 20 cm). Place 30 min in the fridge.
3. Preheat the oven to 180°C (Th. 6), 10 minutes before the end of the cooling time. Bake the pie shell for 15 to 20 minutes. Let cool on rack.
4. Meanwhile, prepare the garnish. In the rinsed and dried bowl, place the dark chocolate and the milk chocolate. Chop 10 sec/speed. 10. Scrape the sides of the bowl with the spatula, then set aside in a salad bowl.
5. Pour the liquid cream into the mixing bowl and heat 3 min/100°C/speed. 1. Pour the hot cream over the chocolate, stir with the spatula, then pour over the bottom of the tart. Place 1 hour in the fridge.
6. Just before serving, put the hazelnuts and decorating sugar in a pan and caramelize for a few minutes. Leave to cool on parchment paper. Coarsely chop the caramelized hazelnuts, then spread them over the surface of the pie.

116. Iced coffee and caramel smoothie

Ingredients for 4 persons :

- ✓ 8 scoops of vanilla ice cream,
- ✓ 100 ml of water,
- ✓ 4 tablespoons of instant coffee (Nescafé),
- ✓ 4 tablespoons of condensed milk,
- ✓ 2 tablespoons of liquid caramel,
- ✓ 100 ml of whiskey cream (baleys type),

Preparation :

1. Start by putting 4 scoops of ice cream, soluble coffee, condensed milk, caramel and whiskey cream in the bowl of your thermomix.

2. Program at speed 4 for 15 seconds.

3. Serve in glasses with a scoop of ice cream in each.

4. Treat yourself.

117. Melon ice cream

Ingredients for 6 people:

- ✓ 400 g of melon (weight once peeled),

- ✓ 80 g of sugar,

- ✓ 250 g of vanilla yogurt,

Preparation :

1. Start by peeling and dicing the melon. Put the melon and the yogurt in the freezer for at least 3 hours.

2. About 5 minutes before you want to prepare our ice cream, take the melon and yogurt out of the freezer.

3. Put the sugar in the bowl of the thermomix and program for 20 seconds at speed 9.

4. Add the melon and yogurt, then cook for 20 seconds at speed 7.

5. Then, program for 20 seconds, speed 4.

6. Serve immediately with a tablespoon of ice cream or a few tablespoons. You can also serve it in glasses.

7. Treat yourself.

118. Chocolate and Rum Ice Cream

Ingredients for 4 persons :

- ✓ 200 g of chocolate for fondant-type desserts,
- ✓ 200 g invert sugar or normal sugar,
- ✓ 150 g of whole milk,
- ✓ 2 eggs,
- ✓ 500 g liquid cream (35% fat),
- ✓ 30 g of rum,

Preparation :

1. Start by putting the chocolate in pieces in the bowl of your Thermomix.

2. Program at progressive speed 5-10 for 10 seconds.

3. Add the sugar, milk and eggs, then set to speed 5 for 6 minutes at 90°C.

4. Then add the liquid cream and the rum, then program at speed 5 for 15 seconds.

5. Pour the contents of the bowl into a metal container and place in the freezer for at least 6 hours.

6. When it is semi-frozen, after about 3 hours, you can cream it even more by putting the ice cream in the bowl of the thermomix and programming for 30 seconds at speed 6. Then put it back in the container

7. and finish freezing it.

8. Serve and enjoy.

119. Chocolate Brownie Ice Cream

Ingredients for 10 people:

- ✓ 175 g of dark chocolate,
- ✓ 300 g of cream,
- ✓ 200 g of milk,
- ✓ 3 egg yolks,
- ✓ 110 g of sugar,
- ✓ 40 g of invert sugar,
- ✓ 1 pinch of salt,
- ✓ 100 g of brownies,

Preparation :

1. Start by putting the chocolate in the bowl of your thermomix and give 2 turbo shots for 2 seconds.
2. Add the cream and set at speed 2 for 4 minutes at 37°C. Remove the melted chocolate and set aside.
3. Insert the butterfly, add the milk, egg yolks, sugar and inverted sugar.
4. Program at speed 4 for 8 minutes at 90°C.
5. Then set to speed 2 and gradually add the melted chocolate and a pinch of salt through the hole in the lid.
6. Pour the contents of the bowl into a container, preferably metal.
7. Place in the freezer for 30 minutes, then remove the container and stir with a spoon or fork to break up the ice crystals.
8. Repeat the same operation 2 more times.
9. Then add the brownie pieces and freeze for at least 2 hours.
10. When ready to serve, take the ice cream out of the freezer and let it cool for a few minutes so that it is softer and creamier.
11. Treat yourself.

120. Light lemon jam with coconut water

Ingredients for 4 persons :

- ✓ 4 lemons,
- ✓ 60 g cooking sweetener,
- ✓ 20 cl coconut water,

Preparation :

1. Start by washing the lemons, then cut them into quarters and remove the seeds.

2. Then put them in a saucepan with the coconut water and add 50 cl of water.

3. Stir everything together, then leave to macerate for 24 hours.

4. After maceration, heat everything and simmer for 30 minutes.

5. Add the sweetener and mix, then boil for 20 minutes.

6. Once the water has evaporated and the jam has set, remove the pan from the heat and divide into jam jars.

121. Chocolate-pear cream flan

Ingredients for 4 Servings:

- ✓ 200g of chocolate,
- ✓ 30 g of vegetable milk,
- ✓ 3 eggs,
- ✓ 250 g of mascarpone,
- ✓ 2 pears,
- ✓ 20 g barley flour,

Preparation :

1. Preheat the oven to 150°C.

2. Put the chocolate in pieces in the bowl of the thermomix and the milk then melt 6min/37°/speed. 2.

3. Add the mascarpone then mix 30 sec/speed 3.

4. Add flour and eggs then mix 30 sec/speed 3.

5. Add the pears cut into pieces then mix 30sec/reverse/speed 2.

6. Transfer to a silicone cake mold and bake for 35 minutes at 150°C. When it comes out of the oven, the flan is still a little soft, that's normal.

7. Leave to cool and set aside for 1 hour in the fridge.

122. Apricot-Coconut Bars with Light Almonds

Ingredients for 30 bars:

- ✓ 115 g of dried apricot,
- ✓ 2 tablespoons of butter,
- ✓ 55 g of honey,
- ✓ 4 tablespoons raw cane sugar,
- ✓ 1 teaspoon of orange zest,
- ✓ 1 tablespoon of orange juice,
- ✓ 115 g spelled flakes,
- ✓ 55 g grated coconut,
- ✓ 4 tablespoons of chopped almonds,

Preparation :

1. Start by chopping the apricots.
2. Bring the butter, honey and sugar to a boil in a small saucepan.
3. Preheat the oven to 150°C.
4. In a salad bowl, mix 1 tablespoon of orange juice, zest, spelled flakes, grated coconut, almonds, diced apricots and butter mixture.
5. Spread the mixture on a baking sheet lined with parchment paper with a dampened rubber spatula until about 1 cm thick.
6. Bake on the middle rack of your oven for about 25 minutes.
7. Remove from the oven and let cool completely before cutting into bars.
8. Serve and enjoy.

123. Light Mango Cheesecake

Ingredients for 10 people:

- ✓ 175 to 200 g of crushed digestive biscuits,
- ✓ 100 g melted unsalted butter,
- ✓ 450 g cream cheese,
- ✓ 180 g fresh cream,
- ✓ 175 g caster sugar,
- ✓ 2 sheets of gelatin,
- ✓ 300 g chopped mango,
- ✓ Mango cut into quarters to garnish,

Preparation :

1. Put the gelatin sheets in a bowl of cold water and let them soften.

2. Combine the crushed digestive biscuits and melted butter in a bowl and press the mixture evenly onto the bottom of the cake pan. Chill in the fridge until ready to fill.

3. Place the cream cheese, double cream and caster sugar in a bowl and whip to soft peaks with an electric whisk. Add the chopped mango.

4. Remove the gelatin sheets from the water, squeeze them well to remove excess water and put them in a small saucepan. Melt over very low heat for one minute. Add some of the cheesecake mixture to the skillet to cool the gelatin, then stir it into the rest of the cheesecake mixture.

5. Pour the cheese mixture over the cookie base and chill in the fridge for 2-3 hours to set. Once set, decorate with the mango slices overlapping them.

6. Serve and enjoy.

124. Strawberries stuffed with Light Cheesecake

Ingredients for 4 persons :

- ✓ 450 to 500 g of fresh strawberries,
- ✓ 220 g cream cheese,
- ✓ 1 teaspoon of stevia,
- ✓ ½ teaspoon of vanilla extract,

Preparation :

1. Start by preparing the strawberries (wash, dry, hull, scoop out the white flesh in the middle with a knife).

2. Cut the cream cheese into pieces, then put it in a bowl and soften it in the microwave for 10 seconds.

3. Then, stir and return to the microwave for 10 more seconds so that it is tender.

4. Once the cream cheese has softened, add the sweetener and vanilla, then whisk until smooth and creamy.

5. Transfer the cream cheese mixture to a piping bag and pipe a small amount into each strawberry.

6. Place in the fridge and take it out 30 minutes before serving.

7. Treat yourself.

125. Pear and brie pie

Ingredients for 6 Servings:

- ✓ 200 g of wheat flour, and a little for the work surface,
- ✓ 20 g of olive oil,
- ✓ 80 g of lukewarm water,
- ✓ ½ tsp. salt,
- ✓ 200 g brie, cut into strips,
- ✓ 2 pears (about 300 g),
- ✓ Ground pepper,
- ✓ 2 – 3 sprigs of fresh thyme (optional),

Preparation :

1. Put the flour, olive oil, water and salt in the bowl, then mix   activates the mixer mode for 1 min. Transfer the dough to a work surface and form a ball. Wrap in cling film and leave to rest for 30 minutes in the fridge.

2. Preheat the oven to 200°C (Th. 6-7). Butter a pie pan and set aside.

3. On a lightly floured work surface, roll out the dough and line the prepared pan. Prick the dough with a fork to avoid the formation of air bubbles. Arrange the Brie on the bottom of the pie and set aside. Cut the pears in half lengthwise and remove the core.

4. Cut half a pear flat side down into slices (1-2 mm), keeping the pear shape. Arrange the sliced pear half in the mold over the brie. Repeat the operation with the other 3 pear halves, arranging them evenly on the tart.

5. Sprinkle with pepper and thyme, then put in the oven and cook for 30 minutes at 200°C.

6. Leave to cool and serve the pie cut into slices.

Cakes

126. Cook'Cake

Ingredients for 8 Servings:

For the cake:
- ✓ 125 g dark chocolate + 10 g coconut oil + 120 g flour + 3 g of bicarbonate,
- ✓ 120 g applesauce + 2 eggs + 25 g chocolate chips,

For the cookies:
- ✓ 110 g flour + 1 pinch of bicarbonate + 1 pinch salt + 70 g coconut oil,
- ✓ 1 tsp vanilla + 1 egg + 50 g chocolate chips,

Preparation :

The cake:
1. Put the chocolate cut into pieces in the bowl of the thermomix then mix 5sec/speed 8. Scrape down sides of bowl with spatula.
2. Add the coconut oil then melt 4min/90°C/reverse/speed 1. Transfer to a bowl and set aside.
3. Wash and dry the bowl.
4. Add the flour to the Thermomix bowl, the baking soda, the eggs and the compote then mix 30sec/speed 3.
5. Add the warm chocolate-coconut oil mix and the chocolate chips then mix 20sec/reverse/speed 2.
6. Transfer to a cake pan. Wash and dry the bowl.
7. Preheat the oven to 180°C.

For cookies:
1. Add the flour to the Thermomix bowl, the baking soda, the salt and the vanilla then mix 20sec/Vit.3.
2. Add coconut oil and egg then mix 20sec./speed 3.
3. Then add the chocolate chips then mix 20sec/reverse/Vit.2.
4. Form balls, flatten them slightly and insert them delicately above the cake batter.
5. Put in the oven for 20 minutes at 180°C.
6. Let cool before unmolding.

127. Healthy Granola

Ingredients for 15 cookies:

- ✓ 110 g of mixed oat flakes,
- ✓ 90 g of semi-complete flour,
- ✓ 20 g almond powder,
- ✓ 1 tsp baking powder,
- ✓ 30 g melted coconut oil,
- ✓ 70 g of almond milk,
- ✓ 100 g of dark chocolate,

Preparation :

1. Preheat the oven to 180°C.

2. Put the oats in the thermomix bowl, the flour, the almond powder and the baking powder then mix 20sec/speed 3.

3. Add milk and coconut oil then mix 20sec/Vit.3.

4. Divide the preparation into cookie cutters to make biscuits with a thickness of 4mm. Place the biscuits on a baking tray, previously covered with baking paper. Put in the oven for 10 min.

5. Let the cookies cool.

6. Place the chocolate cut into pieces in the Thermomix bowl and melt 3min/37°C/speed 3.

7. Coat one side of each biscuit.

8. Place the cookies in the fridge for the chocolate to harden.

128. Apricot cake

Ingredients for 10 Servings:

- ✓ 160 g of wheat flour, and a little for the mold,
- ✓ 50 g butter, cut into pieces,
- ✓ 3 eggs,
- ✓ 1 sachet of vanilla sugar,
- ✓ 1 teaspoon of baking powder (½ sachet),
- ✓ 250 g fresh apricots, quartered,

Preparation :

1. Preheat the oven to 180°C (Th. 6). Butter and flour a cake tin, then set aside.

2. Place butter in mixing bowl and melt 2 min/60°C/speed 2.

3. Add eggs and vanilla sugar then mix 20 sec/speed 3.

4. Add flour and baking powder then mix 30 sec/speed 3. Scrape down sides of mixing bowl with spatula.

5. Then add the apricots and mix 20 sec/speed 2. Transfer to the prepared tin, then place an apricot cut in six on top then put in the oven and cook for 40 minutes at 180°C.

6. Serve warm or chilled.

129. Apple cake and vanilla sugar

Ingredients for 6 Servings:

- ✓ 4 eggs,
- ✓ 30 g of powdered sugar,
- ✓ 170 g of wheat flour,
- ✓ 1 sachet of baking powder,
- ✓ 20 g of neutral oil,
- ✓ 50g of milk,
- ✓ Butter for the dish,
- ✓ 550 g peeled apples, in pieces (about 4),
- ✓ 1 sachet of vanilla sugar,

Preparation :

1. Preheat the oven to 180°C (Th. 6). In the bowl, place the eggs, powdered sugar, flour, baking powder, oil and milk. Mix 30 sec/speed 5.

2. Butter a baking dish, then spread the apples in it. Pour over the previous mixture.

3. Bake for 40 minutes, until the surface of the cake is golden brown.

4. Remove from the oven, sprinkle with vanilla sugar and let cool before eating.

130. Fig and hazelnut cake

Ingredients for 6 Servings:

- ✓ 3 eggs white and yolks separated,
- ✓ 1 natural yoghurt,
- ✓ 30g melted coconut oil,
- ✓ 40g of cornstarch,
- ✓ 1 packet of baking powder,
- ✓ 1 pinch of salt,
- ✓ 100g rolled oats,
- ✓ 1 pinch of cinnamon,
- ✓ 1 tablespoon of almond or hazelnut powder,
- ✓ 60g crushed hazelnuts,
- ✓ 12 figs,

Preparation :

1. Preheat the oven to 180°C.
2. In the bowl, add the egg yolks, plain yogurt, coconut oil, cornstarch, sachet of baking powder, pinch of salt, pinch of cinnamon, oat flakes, ground almonds and the crushed hazelnuts then mix 30sec/Vit.3. Transfer the mixture to a salad bowl and set aside.
3. Wash and dry the thermomix bowl properly.
4. Set up the whisk and insert the egg whites then m mix 3min/speed 3.5. Gently fold the egg whites into the mixture.
5. Cut 8 figs into pieces and 4 figs into quarters.
6. Add the 6 figs to the preparation and pour the preparation into a silicone mold (or previously buttered). Decorate with the remaining figs.
7. Put in the oven for 30 minutes at 180°C.
8. Let cool before unmolding.

131. Spiced carrot cake

Ingredients for 8 Servings:

- ✓ 250 g grated carrots,
- ✓ 100 g ground almonds,
- ✓ 200 g of flour,
- ✓ 3 eggs,
- ✓ 1 tsp. cinnamon,
- ✓ 1 tsp. nutmeg,
- ✓ 25 cl of oil,
- ✓ 1/2 sachet of yeast,
- ✓ 1 pinch of salt,

Preparation :

1. Preheat your oven to 150°C.

2. Put the carrots in the thermomix bowl and mix 5sec/speed 5. Transfer to a bowl and set aside.

3. In the bowl, put the eggs, salt and oil. Mix 1min/speed 4.

4. Add flour, baking powder, cinnamon and nutmeg and mix 30sec/speed 3. Scrape down sides of bowl with spatula and mix again 30 sec/speed 3.

5. Add the grated carrots and the ground almonds then mix 1min/reverse/speed 2.

6. Transfer the preparation into a silicone mold and put in the oven for 40 minutes. Let cool before unmolding.

132. Plum sponge cake

Ingredients for 8 people:

- ✓ 90 g of brown sugar,
- ✓ Zest of a lemon,
- ✓ 150g of flour,
- ✓ 100 g of butter in pieces,
- ✓ 3 eggs,
- ✓ 1 teaspoon of baker's yeast,
- ✓ 7 plums,
- ✓ A handful of dried fruits,

Preparation :

1. Start by putting the brown sugar and lemon zest in the bowl of your thermomix, then set to speed 10 for 10 seconds.
2. Add the flour, butter, eggs and baking powder, then set to speed 4 for 1 minute.
3. Pour the dough obtained into a mold of about 22 cm in diameter. You can use a smaller pan if you want the cake to be taller.
4. Preheat the oven to 180°C.
5. Pit the plums and cut them in half, then scatter them over the cake.
6. Scatter the nuts over the cake and sprinkle a little sugar over the entire surface.
7. Bake for 35 to 40 minutes at 180°C.
8. Once cooked, let cool and store in the fridge until ready to serve.
9. Treat yourself.

133. Crispy Orange Quinoa Cookies

Ingredients for 24 units:

- ✓ 100 g of quinoa flour,
- ✓ 100 g of buckwheat flour,
- ✓ 70 g of candied orange peel,
- ✓ 100 g of butter at room temperature,
- ✓ 100 g of brown sugar,
- ✓ 1 egg,
- ✓ 1 egg yolk,
- ✓ 30 g of whole milk,
- ✓ 1 teaspoon baking powder,
- ✓ Icing sugar for sprinkling,

Preparation :

1. Start by putting the candied orange peels in the bowl of your thermomix and set to speed 6 for 30 seconds.
2. Scrape the sides with a spatula, then add the quinoa and buckwheat flours, the butter, the sugar, the milk, the yeast, the egg and the egg yolk.
3. Program at speed 5 for 1 minute.
4. Remove the dough from the bowl and form a cylinder, then wrap it in cling film and leave to rest in the refrigerator for 30 minutes.
5. Preheat the oven to 160°C. Line 2 baking sheets with parchment paper.
6. Take the dough out of the fridge and divide it into 24 balls, then place them on the sheets, spacing them out and flatten them slightly.
7. Bake for 20 minutes at 160°C.
8. Once cooked, let cool and sprinkle with powdered sugar.
9. Serve and enjoy.

134. Chocolate and almond fondant

Ingredients for 4 Servings:

- ✓ 6 eggs,
- ✓ 50 g butter,
- ✓ A pinch of salt,
- ✓ 230 g of dark chocolate,
- ✓ 120 g almond powder,
- ✓ 1 tbsp vanilla extract,

Preparation :

1. Preheat your oven to 180°C.
2. Start by separating the egg yolks and whites.
3. Then, in the bowl of your Thermomix, put the whisk in place and insert the egg whites and the salt then beat the egg whites until stiff, mixing 4min/speed 3.5. To book. Wash and dry the bowl.
4. Add the chocolate cut into pieces then mix 10 sec/speed 8.
5. Add the soft butter in pieces then melt 4min/55°C/speed 2.
6. At the buzzer add the ground almonds and the egg yolks then mix 20 sec/speed 5.
7. Add the vanilla extract then mix 10 sec/speed 4.
8. Gradually incorporate the beaten egg whites then mix gently with a spatula.
9. Finally, pour the mixture into a silicone mold (or lined with parchment paper).
10. Put in the oven for 30 minutes at 180°C.
11. Let cool before unmolding.

135. Gluten-free Energy Cake

Ingredients for 8 Servings:

- ✓ 2 ripe bananas,
- ✓ 50g of prunes,
- ✓ 150 g of soy milk or other vegetable milk,
- ✓ 20 g of neutral oil,
- ✓ 2 eggs,
- ✓ 60g rolled oats,
- ✓ 180 g of gluten-free mix for pastry (or an almond powder/rice flour mix),
- ✓ 50 g almond powder,
- ✓ 1 sachet of baking powder,
- ✓ 75 g of goji berries,
- ✓ Sliced/whole almonds,

Preparation :

1. Preheat the oven to 170°C.

2. Put the bananas in the thermomix bowl, the soy milk, the oil, the eggs, the oatmeal, the gluten-free mix, the almond powder and the sachet of baking powder then mix 20sec/speed 4.

3. Add the goji berries to the bowl and stir gently with the spatula.

4. Transfer the preparation into a silicone cake mold (or previously buttered) then sprinkle with almonds.

5. Put in the oven for 45min at 170°C.

6. Let cool before unmolding.

136. Walnut and raspberry cupcakes

Ingredients for 10 people:

Genoese :
- ✓ 125 g of melted butter + 25 ml of cream to be assembled,
- ✓ 125g of sugar + 2 eggs + 1 level tablespoon of yeast,
- ✓ 50 g of wheat flour + 50 g of cornstarch,
- ✓ 150 g walnuts + 100 g of raspberries,

Frosting:
- ✓ 40 g of icing sugar + 2 tablespoons of whole milk,

Preparation :

1. Start by mixing the two flours with the baking powder in a bowl, then mix the melted butter with the 25 ml of whipped cream in another bowl.
2. Put 150 g of walnuts in the bowl of your Thermomix and set to speed 6 for 15 seconds. Set the chopped walnuts aside.
3. Without washing the bowl, insert the butterfly and put 2 eggs and 125 g of sugar in it, then set to speed 4 for 6 minutes at 37°C.
4. Then set to speed 4 for 6 minutes.
5. Preheat the oven to 180°C.
6. Add the flour mixture, crushed walnuts and butter mixture to the bowl, then turn to speed 4 for 5 seconds.
7. Spread mini silicone muffin cups with melted butter and fill them halfway with the resulting batter, then put two raspberries inside.
8. Bake for 15 to 18 minutes at 180°C. If you notice the cakes browning too much, cover them with aluminum foil.
9. Once cooked, let them cool in the molds before unmolding.
10. Pour 100 g of icing sugar into a bowl and gradually add the 2 tablespoons of milk while mixing to obtain a glaze.
11. Cover the cupcakes with the frosting and decorate with 2 raspberries.
12. Serve and enjoy.

137. Clafoutis coconut mango and banana

Ingredients for 6 Servings:

- ✓ 75 g of flour,
- ✓ 3 eggs,
- ✓ 85 + 15 g grated coconut,
- ✓ 300 g of coconut milk,
- ✓ 1 mango,
- ✓ 2 bananas,

Preparation :

1. Preheat the oven to 175°C.

2. Put the flour, the eggs and the coconut in the bowl of the Thermomix then mix 30sec/Vit.3. Scrape down sides of bowl with spatula.

3. Put the mango cut into pieces in a gratin dish and the bananas cut into slices.

4. When the bell rings, pour the mixture over the fruit.

5. Put in the oven for 35 minutes at 175°C.

6. Sprinkle with the remaining 15g grated coconut.

7. Serve warm or cold.

138. Gingerbread and apple flavor financial cake

Ingredients for 6 Servings:

- ✓ 1 sachet of vanilla sugar,
- ✓ 60 g almond powder,
- ✓ 50 g of cornstarch,
- ✓ 1/2 tsp gingerbread spice,
- ✓ 3 egg whites,
- ✓ 40 melted butter,
- ✓ 2 apples,
- ✓ Icing sugar,

Preparation :

1. Preheat the oven to 200°C.

2. Put the sugar, the almond powder, the cornstarch and the spices in the bowl of the thermomix then mix 30sec/speed 3.

3. Insert the whisk and insert, through the hole in the lid, onto the running blades, the egg whites and the melted butter. Once the mixture is homogeneous, transfer to a silicone cake mold (or previously buttered).

4. Place the sliced apples on top and press them down lightly.

5. Put in the oven for 35 minutes at 200°C.

6. Leave to cool before deputing then sprinkle with icing sugar.

139. Light Clementine Semolina Cake

Ingredients for 6 people:

- ✓ 5 clementines,
- ✓ 600 g of skimmed milk,
- ✓ 150 g of semolina,
- ✓ 3 eggs,
- ✓ 30 g of brown sugar,
- ✓ 1 tablespoon of vanilla extract,
- ✓ 1 tablespoon of rum,

Preparation :

1. Start by peeling the clementines, then cut them into small pieces.

2. Put the milk in a saucepan and bring it to a boil.

3. Add the sugar, vanilla extract and rum, then mix well.

4. Pour in the semolina while stirring with a whisk for 10 minutes until the preparation thickens.

5. Then beat the eggs into an omelet and add them to the previous preparation.

6. Add the clementines then stir and pour into a silicone cake mold.

7. Preheat the oven to 200°C. Bake for 30 to 35 minutes at 200°C.

8. Once cooked, let cool for a few minutes before unmolding.

9. Serve and enjoy.

140. Banana oatmeal cake

Ingredients for 8 Servings:

- ✓ 250 g of banana + 16 slices of banana for decoration,
- ✓ 1 natural yoghurt,
- ✓ 2 eggs,
- ✓ 80 g oatmeal,
- ✓ 1 tbsp grated coconut,
- ✓ 1 sachet of baking powder,
- ✓ 25 g of dark chocolate,

Preparation :

1. Preheat the oven to 180°C.

2. Place the sliced bananas and yoghurt in the thermomix bowl then chop 5 sec/speed 5.

3. Add eggs, grated coconut, baking powder and dark chocolate then mix 10sec/speed 3.

4. Place the slices of bananas in the bottom of a silicone mold and transfer the preparation on top.

5. Put in the oven for 25 minutes at 180°C.

6. Let cool before unmolding.

141. Fouace

Ingredients for 8 Servings:

- ✓ 145 g of milk,
- ✓ 1 cube of fresh baker's yeast, crumbled,
- ✓ 50 g butter, cut into pieces,
- ✓ 20 g caster sugar,
- ✓ 500 g of wheat flour, and a little flour,
- ✓ 3 eggs,

Preparation :

1. Place 140 g milk and fresh baker's yeast in mixing bowl then heat 1 min 40 sec/37°C/speed 3.

2. Add the butter, sugar, flour and 2 eggs, then activate the 3 min mode/dough mode. Transfer to a floured bowl, cover with cling film and leave to rise for 2 hours at constant temperature.

3. After proving, transfer the dough to a floured work surface. Degas the dough and form a disk the size of the pie pan, then make a hole in the center. Put the crown in the mould, then cover with a tea towel and leave to rise for 30 minutes at a constant temperature.

4. 10 minutes before the end of the rising time, preheat the oven to 180°C (Th. 6).

5. Beat the last egg with the remaining 5 g of milk, then apply the egg wash to the dough using a kitchen brush. Put in the oven and cook for 20-25 minutes at 180°C. Serve warm or chilled.

142. Light yoghurt soft cake

Ingredients for 6 Servings:

- ✓ 4 eggs,

- ✓ 500 g of 0% yoghurt,

- ✓ 100g of flour,

- ✓ 1 tablespoon of vanilla extract,

Preparation :

1. Preheat the oven to 180°C.

2. In the bowl of the thermomix insert the eggs and mix 1min/speed 4.

3. Add flour, yoghurts and vanilla extract then mix 1min/speed 3.

4. Pour the mixture into a silicone mold.

5. Bake for 45 minutes at 180°C.

6. Once out of the oven, let it cool.

7. Tip: You can add 2 tablespoons of agave syrup.

8. You can accompany this cake with fresh fruit.

143. Chocolate peanut cookie

Ingredients for 20 Pieces:

- ✓ 100 g dry roasted peanuts, salted,
- ✓ 1 sachet of vanilla sugar,
- ✓ 50 g butter, cut into pieces,
- ✓ 1 egg,
- ✓ 50 g of wheat flour,
- ✓ 1 teaspoon of baking powder (½ sachet),
- ✓ 3 pinches of vanilla powder,
- ✓ 100 g of chocolate chips,

Preparation :

1. Preheat the oven to 180°C (Th. 6). Line 2 baking sheets with baking paper and set aside.
2. Place peanuts in mixing bowl and chop 5 sec/speed 4.
3. Add vanilla sugar, butter, egg, flour, baking powder and vanilla powder then mix 20 sec/speed 4.
4. Add chocolate chips and mix 10 sec/reverse/speed 3. Using 2 tbsp. coffee, form balls and distribute them on the prepared plates, making sure to space them 5 cm apart.
5. Place in the oven and cook for 15-20 minutes at 180°C, until the biscuits are golden brown. Cool on a wire rack before serving, or store in an airtight container.
6. Tips: For more consistent cookies, roll a ball of dough in the palm of your hand and flatten it slightly on the baking sheet.

144. Coconut and cherry cake

Ingredients for 10 Servings:

- ✓ 250 g pitted cherries,
- ✓ 250 g of 20% of white cheese
- ✓ 60 g grated coconut,
- ✓ 250 g of fluid flour,
- ✓ 1 packet of baking powder,
- ✓ 3 eggs,
- ✓ 1 tsp lemon juice,

Preparation :

1. Preheat the oven to 160°C.

2. Then in the bowl of your thermomix, put the eggs, and the lemon juice, then mix 2min/Vit.2.

3. Add the flour, baking powder and white cheese, then mix 1 min/speed 1.

4. Add cherries and coconut, mix 2min/reverse/speed 1.

5. Finally, pour the preparation obtained into a silicone mold and put in the oven for 45 minutes at 160°C.

6. Let cool before unmolding.

145. Brownie without butter

Ingredients for 8 Servings:

- ✓ 5 g of neutral oil,
- ✓ 50 g of wheat flour, and a little for the mold,
- ✓ 150g apples, quartered,
- ✓ 200 g dark chocolate 70% cocoa, broken into pieces,
- ✓ 3 eggs,
- ✓ 50 g of pecan nuts or walnuts and hazelnuts,

Preparation :

1. Preheat the oven to 180°C (Th. 6), lightly oil and flour a cake tin (Ø 24 cm), then set aside.

2. Place apples and chocolate in mixing bowl then chop 5 sec/speed 5. Scrape down sides of mixing bowl with spatula.

3. Cook 10 min/90°C/speed 2, then blend 10 sec/speed 5.

4. Add flour and eggs to mixing bowl then mix 30 sec/speed 4. Pour mixture into prepared tin, decorate with pecan nuts or walnut and hazelnut kernels, then place in the oven and cook for 15-20 minutes at 180 °C.

5. Leave to cool before eating.

146. Crown with apple and lemon

Ingredients for 8 Servings:

- ✓ 200 g apples, cut into slices (2-3 mm),
- ✓ 1 untreated lemon,
- ✓ 50 g butter, cut into pieces and a little for the mold,
- ✓ 150 g of wheat flour, and a little for the mold,
- ✓ 1 sachet of vanilla sugar,
- ✓ 3 eggs,
- ✓ 1 teaspoon of baking powder (½ sachet),
- ✓ 20 g of rum,
- ✓ 1 teaspoon of natural vanilla extract,
- ✓ 1 tsp. cinnamon powder (optional),

Preparation :

1. Put the apple slices in a container. Zest and squeeze the lemon, reserve the zest, pour the juice over the apples, then mix with the spatula.
2. Preheat the oven to 180°C (Th. 6). Butter and flour a savarin mold (Ø 25 cm), then set aside.
3. Place sugar and lemon zest in mixing bowl then grind 10 sec/speed 10. Scrape down sides of mixing bowl with spatula.
4. Add flour, butter, eggs, baking powder, rum and vanilla extract then mix 1 min/speed 4. Transfer to prepared tin and spread evenly with spatula. Arrange the reserved apple slices on top, either flat or upright, pressing them lightly into the batter. If necessary, sprinkle the cake with cinnamon, then put in the oven and cook for 30-35 minutes at 180°C.
5. Check for doneness with a knife blade, which should come out clean. Allow cake to cool in pan for about 10 minutes before unmolding. Serve warm or cold.

147. Fondant cake with pears and chocolate chips

Ingredients for 8 Servings:

- ✓ 100 g of wheat flour, and a little for the mold,
- ✓ 2 eggs,
- ✓ 1 pinch of salt,
- ✓ 50 g ground almonds,
- ✓ 1 teaspoon of baking powder (½ sachet),
- ✓ 100g of milk,
- ✓ 3 tablespoons of neutral oil,
- ✓ 70 g of dark chocolate chips,
- ✓ 3 to 4 pears, cut into strips,

Preparation :

1. Preheat the oven to 180°C (Th. 6).

2. Place eggs and salt in mixing bowl then blend 20 sec/speed 5.

3. Add flour, ground almonds, baking powder, milk and oil then mix 10 sec/speed 5.

4. Add chocolate chips and mix 10 sec/speed 2. Line the prepared mold with half of the dough, arrange the pears evenly on the surface, then add the rest of the dough. Put in the oven and cook for 40 minutes at 180°C.

5. Remove from oven and allow to cool in pan before serving.

148. Light Brookies

Ingredients for 12 servings:

For the brownies:
- ✓ 80 g dark chocolate,
- ✓ 2 eggs,
- ✓ 60 g of flour,
- ✓ 2 tablespoons of sweetener,
- ✓ 2 tablespoons of oil,
- ✓ 20 g crushed walnuts,

For cookies:
- ✓ 30 g of chocolate chips,
- ✓ 100 g flour,
- ✓ 1 egg,
- ✓ 2 tablespoons of sweetener,
- ✓ 2 tablespoons light butter,
- ✓ 1/2 teaspoon baking powder,

Preparation :

1. For the preparation of the brownies:
2. Start by melting the chocolate with 2 tablespoons of oil in the microwave.
3. In a bowl beat 2 eggs with the sweetener then add the melted dark chocolate and mix.
4. Then add the flour and mix.
5. Then pour into a mold and smooth the top with a spatula.
6. For the preparation of the cookie:
7. In a bowl, mix the butter with the sweetener and mix well.
8. Add flour and baking powder and mix well.
9. Add the nuggets and mix everything together.
10. Then gently flatten the dough end by end on the brownie batter.
11. Preheat the oven to 180°C.
12. Bake for about 20 to 25 minutes at 180°C.

149. Oatmeal and almond muffins

Ingredients for 8 Pieces:

- ✓ 150 g rolled oats,

- ✓ 100 g of applesauce,

- ✓ 1 egg,

- ✓ 60 g crushed almonds,

Preparation :

1. Preheat the oven to 180°C.

2. Add the oatmeal, compote, egg and almonds to the thermomix bowl then mix 30 sec/speed 3.

3. Divide the mixture into muffin tins.

4. Put in the oven for 15 minutes at 180°C.

5. Variation: Replace almonds with hazelnuts.

150. Kit Kat brownies

Ingredients for 6 Servings:

- ✓ 150 g of dark chocolate,

- ✓ 50 g of butter,

- ✓ 45 g of flour,

- ✓ 1 teaspoon of yeast,

- ✓ 3 eggs,

- ✓ 5 Kit Kat cookies,

Preparation :

1. Preheat the oven to 180°C.

2. Put the dark chocolate in pieces in the Thermomix bowl then chop 10sec/speed 7.

3. Add the butter then set 4min./50°C/speed 2.

4. Add flour, eggs and baking powder then mix 30 sec/speed 4.

5. Butter and flour a mold then pour half of the preparation.

6. Top with Kit Kat cookies and cover with remaining batter.

7. Bake for 20 to 25 minutes at 180°C.

Printed in Great Britain
by Amazon

12911757R00099